THIS IS OUR HOME

*a sustainability story to help you start
your own **eco-friendly journey***

trent a. romer

Birdwatch Publishing

news@trentromer.com

ISBN: 979-8-218-17049-3 (paperback)
ISBN: 979-8-218-17140-7 (ebook)
ISBN: 979-8-218-17141-4 (audiobook)

Ordering Information:
Special discounts are available on quantity purchases by corporations, associations, and others. For details, visit https://trentromer.com/contact or email news@trentromer.com

To the people of Nassau New York

You have helped me reflect, persevere and be thankful

CONTENTS

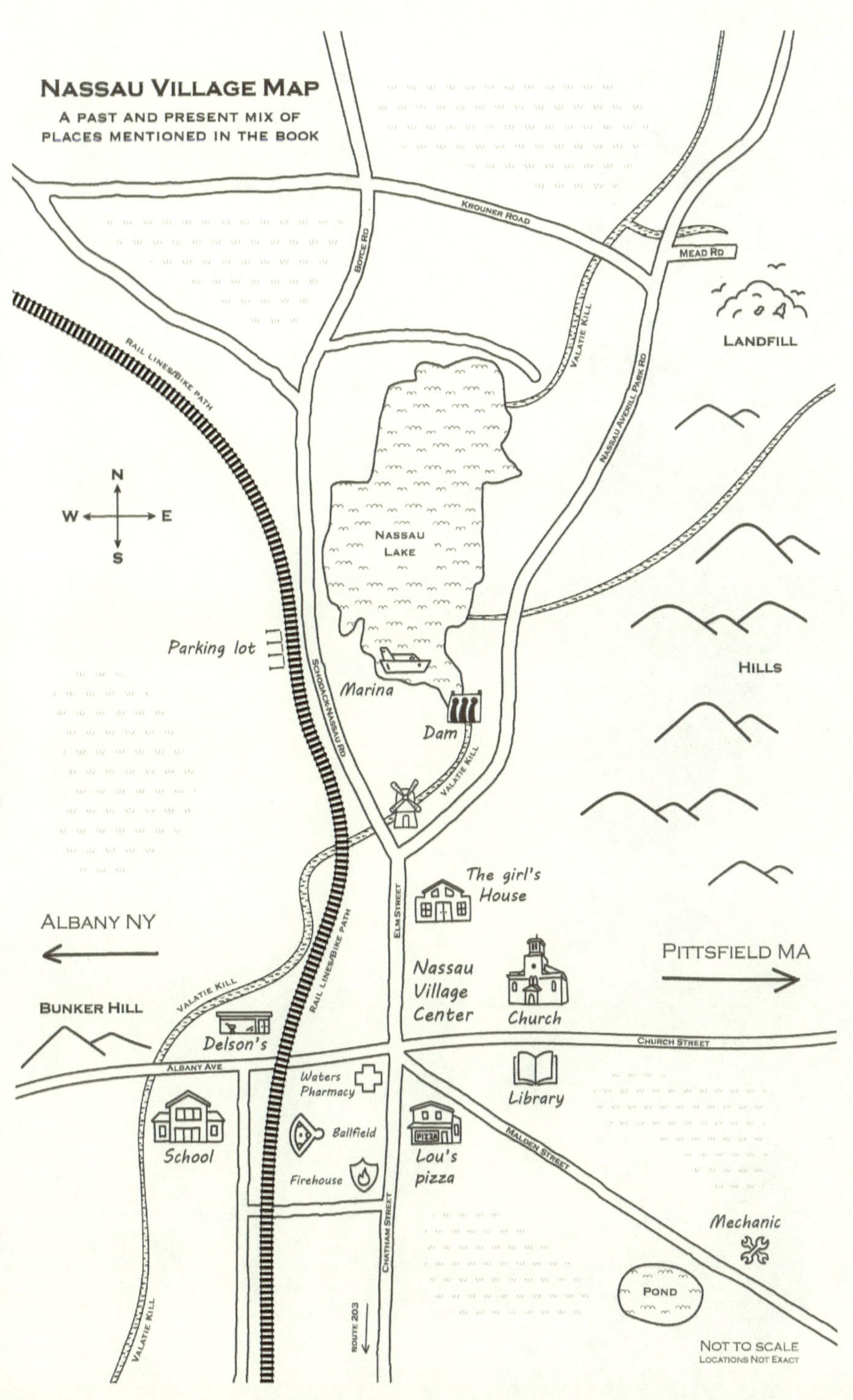

NASSAU VILLAGE MAP
A PAST AND PRESENT MIX OF PLACES MENTIONED IN THE BOOK
KROUNER ROAD
BORCE RD
MEAD RD
VALATIE KILL
NASSAU AVERILL PARK RD
LANDFILL
RAIL LINES/BIKE PATH
N
W E
S
Nassau Lake
HILLS
Parking lot
SCHODACK-NASSAU RD
Marina
Dam
VALATIE KILL
ALBANY NY
PITTSFIELD MA
The girl's House
ELM STREET
RAIL LINES/BIKE PATH
VALATIE KILL
BUNKER HILL
Nassau Village Center
Church
Delson's
CHURCH STREET
ALBANY AVE
Waters Pharmacy
Library
Ballfield
MALDEN STREET
School
Firehouse
Lou's pizza
PIZZA
Mechanic
CHATHAM STREET
POND
ROUTE 203
NOT TO SCALE
LOCATIONS NOT EXACT

INTRODUCTION

A teenage girl floats in the middle of the lake, waiting anxiously. Her ski tips up, body in a crouch, life jacket straps gouging her armpits. She watches intently as the motorboat quickly takes the slack of the rope. As the rope tightens, so do her nerves and muscles. Though getting up on the skis has become routine, she has never quite got used to the adrenaline rush, just before the rope pulls taut.

About three miles away a truck carrying barrels of chemicals rumbles east down Bunker Hill along Route 20 toward the village. The steep decline allows the driver to coast to the main intersection in town. The truck waits to turn left. Walkers and bikers crossing the street are his primary sources of delay. The truck driver sees stores, a barber shop, postal workers, and road construction signs. He watches as kids hurry to catch up with their parents. The sights and sounds of a busy village center fill his cabin.

The ski rope whips out of the water as the boat accelerates, lifting the girl to her feet. Her uneasiness just seconds prior is replaced by exhilaration as the wind blows her hair and water droplets peel away from her body. A sense of calm comes over her as she settles in behind the boat on the cloudless mid-summer day.

The truck, with its barrels of chemicals, turns left onto Elm Street, where the girl lives. It passes her house and follows the road directly north, lumbering over a small bridge. The stream flowing under the bridge originates from the southern end of the lake.

The girl begins to move in and out of the wake, which widens her view to beyond the back of the boat. Sailboats, canoes, and people sitting outside restaurants that line the shore draw her attention. The rush of the wind and the hum of the motor 50 feet in front of her drown out all other sound. A faint smell of gas from the boat mingles with the fresh air. She feels hot sun on her back. The boat heads south toward the marina.

The truck now heads north away from the village. It climbs a small hill and then gains speed as it descends the other side. In less than a mile, the truck will pass the marina and hug the shoreline on the west side of the lake. The lake will be just a few feet away on the passenger side.

The boat approaches the marina and banks hard left at top speed, slinging the girl far outside the wake toward the shore and the parallel road.

The girl sees the truck.

The driver of the truck sees her.

The girl imagines they are on a collision course—but it's an illusion, like an airplane flying in front of the sun.

They intersect for just a moment and then continue their own paths. The girl loops back toward the middle of the lake. The truck follows the road before disappearing as the road and shoreline diverge.

I imagined this scene as I sat in my kayak in the middle of that same lake. I floated where the girl may have crouched on her skis 70 years ago.

What did the girl know about the truck? What did the truck driver know about the barrels it carried? Who filled the barrels and what did they know about their contents? Did the people in the village know where the truck was heading with its cargo?

I had no answers to these questions.

The lake had been silent for all 50 years of my life.

In some ways, the silence had a calming effect. Sunlight drenched the water, reflecting off the waveless surface, and forcing my sunglasses off my head and onto my nose. A gentle breeze stirred the warm air, creating a perfect recipe for comfort. Peace filled my boat. A picture-postcard scene.

In other ways, the silence was troubling. There was no other activity on the water—no boats, no swimmers, no skiers, no fishing, no sailing. I was alone on this bright, summer Saturday. I wanted to appreciate the silence, but I knew better.

The lack of activity on the lake spoke to an invisible threat. To the past that affected the present. After 50 years of ignoring the lake, it was time to give it my full attention.

There were secrets. Secrets the lake wanted to tell.

In a race against time and a quest to find sustainability, the lake offered wisdom and hope of understanding—if I cared to listen.

Who is in the boat? That is the most common question I get from my first book, *Finding Sustainability*. The cover depicts a lone person kayaking on a calm lake with mountain peaks in the background. The dominant color is blue. Varying hues define the water, shoreline, mountains, and sky. The net effect offers a silent, soothing, and serene setting for the lone figure. The question seemed random at first, but eventually enough people asked that I paid more attention.

Why were people asking it? Was it pure curiosity? Maybe, but I suspect it was something deeper. People often assumed the person on the cover was me. I, however, had hoped that readers would see themselves as the one in the boat charting their own journey toward sustainability.

If the person in the boat was my analogy to sustainability being an individual choice and a means to join a larger movement, then the assumption that the person was me showed me my message was not being received as I'd intended. If I thought of myself as an educator, I had to reflect on an old truism—if the student is not learning, the teacher is not teaching.

If everyone thinks sustainability is someone else's job, then they do not see themselves as part of the solution, and the challenge to find sustainability grows.

This reality put me back to work. I looked deeper into what I wrote, how I wrote it, and what I could do better to help the sustainability movement. If the movement could generate enough momentum, sustainability would begin to roll downhill on its own as the primary framing of everyday design, decisions, and dialogue.

This book attempts to show what can happen when we overlook sustainability. I write it through my own lens: as a child who grew up near a toxic dump and polluted lake, as an adult who spent 30 years in the plastic bag manufacturing business, and as a family man who loves nature and wants to pursue a circular future.

I want to share some new things I've learned about sustainability. Deeper than that, my hope is to challenge you, dear reader, in a new way.

My goal with this book is to help you realize you too have a boat and a sustainability journey to explore. You too have a choice. Each choice we make has enormous consequences.

Two confounding obstacles stand in the way of boarding the boat:

1. Compelling reasons to get in

2. Clear plans on what to do once you're in

If we can adopt a new mindset around sustainability, we can uncover a confidence with limitless reserves. Thought changes understanding, tolerances, and actions. Knowledge provides personal power. Applying it empowers others.

The time is now. As we wait, the sands in the bottom of the hourglass accumulate. We can no longer simply turn it upside down to start the time again.

The sustainability movement is a great puzzle with millions and millions of pieces. Each of us owns a piece, including me.

And each piece is itself a puzzle. Each of us must first put together our individual puzzle before we contribute it to the larger mosaic.

Hopefully this book provides you with insights and ideas, motivation, and muscle to take on the challenge of putting your own puzzle together. For the greater good, yes. And to see yourself as the one in the boat.

Chapter 1

SHOCK EVENTS AND BEING CONNECTED

My wife and I pulled our car off to the side of the paved road. A chain extended the width of the road to prevent vehicles from going any further. On either side of the road massive white pine trees stretched toward the sky.

We walked the remaining distance to the potential site of our first house. The square lot was in a heavily wooded area, a small sign that read "Lot 13" the only marking. We hadn't set out to build a house, but after searching for months, we opened our minds to the possibility.

The builder was about to open the second phase of the development. We had driven through the first phase, which showed beautiful homes on wooded lots, houses sitting peacefully among the trees. There were no fences and little ornamental landscaping. The woods provided beauty and a natural barrier between properties.

We fell in love with the neighborhood that day. My wife and I knew this would be the place to raise our family.

We signed a "lot hold" and building on our new home began a few months later. We asked to keep as many trees as possible, especially the white pines. The pines' towering size projected resilience to achieving maturity and the number that had grown together emanated strength and gave us a sense of protection. The magnetism of the trees drew us in, and we knew we wanted to live among them.

The pines seemed to offer the first clue to us moving in a sustainable direction.

The eastern white pine is the largest conifer native to the eastern United States. They can grow to 150 feet—as fast as two feet per year—with trunk diameters of up to 40 inches. Some live for over 200 years.[1]

The trees seek the light from an opening in the canopy above to grow straight up. On mature trees, branches only grow on the upper half of the trunk. The tall trunks and their horizontal, upturned branches stretch to the sky. Today, from the road, our house is visible beneath the branches. Our roof is not.

The evergreens keep their leaves through the winter. Though they are commonly referred to as pine needles, they are in fact very skinny leaves that serve the same function as leaves on a maple or elm tree.[2]

The surrounding deciduous trees' barren appearance in winter pushes the eastern white pines to the front of the landscape stage to face the season alone.

In high winds, the trunks bend and the branches above sway back and forth like drunken sailors holding one another up. From above it must appear like wind rippling through a field of giant wildflowers.

It's nerve-racking when the winds get up as the mature pines could hit our house if they fell the right way.

In fact, in our first year of living there, those nerves were tested when three pines came down. Two fell in the backyard and one shaved the back of the house. One foot closer and the tree would have found our upstairs bathroom.

When the tree removal company came, they told us something fascinating: trees like this move together. They grow together over many, many years and draw strength from one another. They withstand the weather together. They "listen" to each other.

Science supports this idea. According to an article in *Smithsonian Magazine*, trees do so much more than compete or even coexist.

The article describes the widely assumed and accepted view of trees as being loners, battling for water, soil, nutrients, and sunlight. The winners overshadow the losers, "sucking them dry." But there is now a substantial body of evidence that refutes this idea. Trees' root systems, underground fungal networks, and leaves all share nutrients, water, and even distress signals in the air about danger, drought, and disease.[3]

Underground, there are "infinite biological pathways that connect trees," says Suzanne Simard in her TED Talk, "How Trees Talk to Each Other." Simard is a Canadian scientist and professor at the University of British Columbia. She provides evidence that forests communicate to allow them to act like a connected, larger, single organism with an intelligence of sorts.[4]

It turned out that when the developer removed some trees to build our house, it weakened the surrounding forest.

I asked the tree surgeon how many more would fall.

"How many are within 75 feet of the house?" he responded.

This was a sobering comment, as more than 20 pines could potentially qualify. He did also say, however, that once the weaker ones fell, the trees would find a new equilibrium with the new house and would settle.

Twenty years later, he was right. We have not had any trees fall since.

As I look out the back of our house to the white pines blowing together in the wind, I am reminded of how connected they are. When something happens to one, it affects them all.

What I learned while writing *Finding Sustainability* was that the paths of survival and of preservation did not have to be mutually exclusive in our 60-year-old family-owned and operated plastic bag manufacturing company.

I knew plastics were important in many aspects of our everyday lives. I was also acutely aware of the major environmental problems they caused. There is too much unnecessary plastic being manufactured; they are mainly made from fossil fuels, and more and more plastics are winding up in the natural environment with negative effects on wildlife, lands, waterways, and oceans.

In 2018, a growing public anti-plastic narrative combined with my own long-standing, festering, uneasy conscience about the product we made put me at a crossroads both personally and professionally.

One path led to preservation of the planet, the other to survival of my livelihood. How could I do both? Was it even possible?

To survive financially, I might have to sacrifice the preservation of the environment. To play my part in preserving the planet, I might have to sacrifice our company. I pondered this until my mind saw a third option where the path on land split to either preservation or survival—a boat on the shore of a body of water. The fictitious boat in the water offered an alternative that led to education, feedback, and actions in a more sustainable direction.

Sustainability allows us to both *survive in* and *preserve* the environment.

THE POWER OF SHOCKING EVENTS

The word sustainability began to gain prominence in the 1980s. In 1983 the former Prime Minister of Norway, Gro Harlem Brundtland, was chosen by the United Nations to chair the World Commission on Environment and Development. The aim of the commission was to unite countries in the pursuit of sustainable development. In 1987, the Brundtland Commission, as it was then called, published a report titled "Report of the World Commission on Environment and Development: Our Common Future." It attempted to link the issues of economic development and environmental stability.

The report provided the most often used definition of sustainable development as "development that meets the needs of the present without compromising the ability of future generations to meet their own needs."[5]

While the definition is vague, it does tie into the idea of

intergenerational equity. Pure survival benefits only current generations. Pure preservation helps only the future. The challenge is finding the shade of gray between the extremes.

At the end of my previous book, I vowed to return to land in my sustainability boat to help those who felt as conflicted as I once did. My duty to them is to keep learning, share information, and encourage others to get into their boats and find their own way to sustainability where they can both survive and help to preserve. Without a visible or urgent need, people are less likely to get into their boats.

Shock events can cause real change. These are events that are so severe, so acute, that the majority of people recognize things need to change fast.

The Covid-19 pandemic has changed healthcare for years to come. Medical supply chains will seek more domestic sources to avoid over-reliance on imports; funding toward virus research will increase; telehealth will become normal; and we hope for a renewed interest in people joining the medical profession.[6]

The Hayman Fire in 2002 was the largest and most damaging wildfire in Colorado history at the time: 138,000 acres were burned, 600 structures were lost, and over 5,000 people had to evacuate their homes with 14,000 more on standby. The fire raged for a month and resulted in huge change.

Change that spiked collaboration of local, state, and federal agencies with individual citizens to promote mitigation efforts on their land. Change that lessened the resistance to projects conducted by public entities for fire prevention. Change that paved the way for laws like the Healthy Forest Restoration Act (HFRA) and funding to allow for a freer flow of investment toward prevention.[7]

In yet another example, Hurricane Andrew created immediate change. The 1992 hurricane hammered Miami-Dade County, flattening buildings and houses. After the storm, laws were passed to be better able to cope if it were to happen again. Four hundred separate building codes in the state became one uniform code that is updated every three years. The new code more accurately called out exterior building requirements to help withstand high winds and flooding. Requirements like building windows stronger, reinforcing grates and ensuring they are bolted down, and fortifying existing or new foundations with cement blocks instead of wood.[8] Regulations also required supermarkets, gas stations, and hospitals to be equipped with generators.[9]

Unlike Covid-19, the Hayman Fire, and Hurricane Andrew, the climate crisis will likely not manifest as one singular shock event to fundamentally change the way we interact with nature. The loss of biodiversity, rising global temperatures, and the escape of chemicals and materials into the natural environment all happen at a hidden pace, in varying amounts, and in different places at different times.

The abundance of these environmental events disperses consensus on their cause and thereby cripples action. Without a singular shock event, making real change becomes more elusive and makes the march toward crisis more likely. The longer it takes, the more time is wasted, which means more damage. Damage that will potentially be irreversible by the time our collective consciousness realizes acute action is needed.

Like the tall eastern pines' need to move together to survive, we are all tied to one another in our need to positively affect the planet. No one tree nor one person can do it alone, yet each plays a starring role. No one shocking environmental event will likely cause unified urgency of action.

The obstacles are daunting without knowledge and only grow larger when the will to change is absent. With knowledge and will working together, getting into the boat moves from optional to urgent.

So, let's go. The sands in the hourglass continue to fall. The next grain will not wait for us nor the next after that. This story must be told to chart a new course, give us more time.

To tell this story, we start in a small town feeling the lasting effects of a catastrophic environmental event. This town could be any town and any town could be this town—but this place happens to be my own hometown.

Chapter 2

COMMUNITY

Every Thursday when I was 12, I got off the school bus, loaded newspapers into my bag, and mounted my Huffy Pro Thunder BMX bicycle. My paper route, delivering the *Chatham Courier*, a weekly paper focused on local stories, navigated the streets of my hometown of Nassau, New York.

Nassau is a small town in eastern New York midway between Albany, New York to the west, and the Massachusetts border to the east. The town is around 45 square miles with 4,800 residents. The village of Nassau sits within the town and is approximately 1 square mile with 1,100 residents. This is where I grew up.

The village has one streetlight at its center where five roads meet—the main east/west thoroughfare is joined by three country roads feeding into it. Albany Avenue and Church Street connect to form the main road while Chatham Street, Malden Street, and Elm Street spoke off the intersection. Our house was midway down Elm Street.

My newspaper bag had a wide, double-stitched orange strap that extended about two feet above the canvas bag. The bag was stiff and a bright beige when I signed on to become a carrier 11 months before. Now, the weight of the papers and variable weather conditions had softened the fabric and darkened the color.

I was more focused on staying upright than I was on avoiding puddles, so mud often spit up at me during the ride. Ink from the papers rubbed into the canvas and the bag periodically grated against the back tire, so it constantly bore fresh markings. The weathered canvas gave off an aroma of newsprint, fabric, and mildew to formulate its own paperboy musk.

I'd sling the wide strap over my head with the empty bag resting on my hip, the strap like a bandolier across my chest. Then I'd load 20 papers into the bag. The weight of them forced me to lean to the opposite side for balance—body on the left of the bike, sack and papers on the right.

Once loaded, off I went. Had I been stronger or older, or a combination of the two, I could have carried more than 20 papers at a time, which would have saved me numerous trips home to reload to finish my route. My skinny legs did all they could to keep the wheels turning and I always longed to get through the first few houses to lighten the load.

Between deliveries, I wandered into local stores or stopped to chat with villagers.

Mr. Waters was the local pharmacist. I loved to pop into his store and talk sports. He was a fountain of baseball history and statistics, and I was a thirsty listener. He had an enclosed baseball pitching machine at his house and he gave me an open invitation for hitting pointers and practice. I went often. He was a kind, patient man as well as a trusted medical professional in our small village.

Down the street from the pharmacy was Delson's mini department store. It was the Walmart before Walmart. Groceries, hammers, shoelaces, kites, nail polish remover, beach towels, slinkies, and camping gear all under one roof. Their slogan was "If we don't have it, you don't need it."[10] The toy aisle was always an easy justification for a quick stop.

South of the main traffic light sat Delaney's convenience store with its extensive penny candy section. Over the course of my childhood, I could count 5,000 Swedish fish and 500 packs of baseball cards on the low side of my purchases.

The sleigh-riding hill behind the Catholic church was a short walk east of the main intersection. In winter I was always tempted to drop my bag and join the fun as I rode or walked by, but I knew I had to finish my route.

Many of my customers lived on Elm Street—my street. The same street the truck with the barrels drove down years before. Sidewalks, streetlights, and mature trees ran parallel to the road, the trees serving as enormous umbrellas for the pavement below. It took two kids interlocking hands to complete the circumference of the tree trunks. Each week the majesty of these trees projected strength that found a way to my legs and gave me the energy to complete my route.

My customers were only drop-off points unless I had to collect money, which I usually did on Sunday evenings as this seemed to be the best time to find people in their homes.

Most houses on the route were easy, but there was one house in particular that always gave me trouble: the Prusky residence. The people were very nice, but the Doberman Pinscher, that stood nearly as tall as I did, used to strike the utmost fear in me as I approached the house.

In the summer, the storm door with screens in the panels was closed, but the inside door was always open to cool the house. As I prepared to knock, I knew the huge dog would run to the door. He barked and growled, white fangs bared. He pushed against the door to try to get out and, I truly believed, eat me. Thick saliva dripped from his jaws like icicles off a rooftop.

"It's the paperboy," I heard Mr. Prusky say. I knew the next 30 to 60 seconds were critical to my survival: the Doberman on one side of a thin metal screen door and me on the other, my body weight pressed against the outside frame, a death grip on the handle.

"Don't worry about him, he won't hurt you," called out Mrs. Prusky as she searched for payment. My mind heard the phrase but edited out the "don't" and the "won't" part. As each second ticked by, the dog grew more frustrated that he hadn't yet sunk his teeth into me.

"Be right there," she added. I tried soothing "dog" talk, but that had no effect.

When Mrs. Prusky finally came to the door, we exchanged pleasantries, and the dog became docile. The door was cracked ever so slightly to allow the money and receipt to be traded while keeping the dog inside. With the exchange made and the door closed, the dog gave me one last look as if to say, "I'll see you in a month. I'll be ready."

I walked away triumphant but wary of our next meeting.

While I dreaded doing it, I always felt good when I was done collecting for two reasons.

First were the tips. My customers were generous, especially around Christmas.

Second was something I did not recognize at the time but became very clear to me later in life. In our brief exchanges, month after month, I grew to know them, and they knew me.

They were my customers, but they also doubled as faith formation leaders, schoolteachers, volunteer firemen, store owners, librarians, or sports coaches. We grew an invisible bond. This bond combined with countless others in the town, formed just like mine. The net effect was a spider web of support—invisible, strong, resilient.

As a boy, I did not understand what the web represented. I just knew I was cared for and looked after. Equally, I didn't see my hometown as anything more than the place I lived and the points on my route where I delivered newspapers. As an adult, I now recognize the whole is greater than the sum of those parts—it's the definition of a community.

Nassau was my whole world growing up—it contained all I needed and seemed to have anything anyone could need. The self-contained village had it all within a five-minute walk of the main intersection.

Church Street headed east towards Massachusetts. An antique store and the preschool I attended as a toddler was on the left with a dine-in restaurant across the street. A little further up was the town clerk, town court, and village library surrounded by three historic churches—Catholic, Methodist, and the one I attend, Reformed. Across the street from the Catholic church just off the main road was a florist shop.

Albany Avenue fed into the intersection from the city of Albany 15 miles to the west. The town pharmacy, a barber shop, a dentist, an optometrist, a salon, the liquor store, a gun store, a bank, a small hotel with just a few rooms, a synagogue, a convenience store, Delson's department store, a lawyer's office, a mechanic, and a hardware store dotted the sides of the road. The elementary school sat atop a hill a block off Albany Avenue. I walked to school every day from kindergarten through 4th grade.

Malden and Chatham Streets V'd off the main road headed south—one led to the post office, meat market, auto mechanic, and ice-skating pond. The other to the firehouse, Delaney's penny candy store, a VFW, the Little League field, and a cemetery about a mile out. In the center of the V was Lou's Pizza Hub.

Lou made a great authentic pizza. He was a big burly guy who spoke with an accent foreign to my 12-year-old ears. He was direct and he was kind. The hair missing from the top of his head could be seen escaping from his ears and nose. He always wore a white apron that ballooned a bit at his waistline. Every day he stood behind the small counter taking orders, answering the phone, kneading dough, watching ovens, and boxing pies and he did it all without a stitch of panic.

On a hot summer day, going to Lou's with $2.50, found through a combination of searching under the couch cushions, raiding the spare change cup, and sneaking into my mom's purse, would net me two slices of pizza hot from the oven and a jumbo soda with crushed ice filling half the cup. With just a few tables in the small restaurant and the air conditioning cranked, we filled our bellies with goodness and watched Lou as he performed his magic.

The final intersecting street was Elm Street, which headed north out of town. Near the intersection were a gas station, bank, and funeral home with an insurance company operating out of a house and a small pen factory further up. The rest of the street was residential homes—our house was midway down on the right.

As a kid I did not recognize what had to have happened prior to allow these places to exist. I know now that a big part of progress is investment. Investment of time, resources, and effort for longer-term value. Investment in Nassau over the years provided an environment for small businesses to thrive and a surrounding all-inclusive community to grow. A lack of investment is like a series of landmines that go off in varying ways over the long term. With fewer shops to patronize, churches to attend, community activities to participate in, and jobs to fill, people seek those opportunities elsewhere at the expense of the local community.

If investment is crucial to long-term community, then what sort of factors prevent investment? The best way I could think of to understand why investment slows and witness its eroding effects was to visit places and talk to people who have experienced it first-hand. Traveling to these places to gain a more complete perspective became a priority as my journey progressed.

Being outside and interacting with neighbors and villagers was part of daily life. We kids filled our days with stick ball, football, swimming, wiffle ball, basketball, tennis, exploring the woods behind the house, four square, picking raspberries and blackberries, and riding our bikes around the village.

Our moonlight hours were consumed by playing neighborhood chase, catching fireflies, sleepovers, looking for night crawlers, walking to get ice cream, and playing board games.

Nassau was my bubble growing up. There was not much

reason to venture outside the bubble—nor a means to do so. Being outside all day with access to all parts of the village was independence at its best. Our days were timed by an early morning phone call from friends, a quick good-bye to Mom, and a dinner bell calling us home hours later. What happened in between was seemingly not an issue with our parents.

Community then was in-person, hands-on, and natural.

Today, in many ways, community has changed its form. The digital age has reduced in-person contact, allowing for ease of organizing teams and events and offering quick advice for any number of situations. It has also opened a window into the perils of "what could happen if kids are unattended."

I played Little League baseball in my community. My sons played for a travel team after a few years in community baseball. I played outside most days. My sons play inside a lot of the time. I knocked on my friends' doors to play. My sons direct message theirs. I went to the arcade to play video games. My kids play online. I was allowed to roam the neighborhood with few questions asked. My wife and I allow our kids to play in the neighborhood only after a series of helicopter parent questions have been duly answered—who will be there, where are you going, what are you going to do, and when will you be home.

If I had what they had—movies, videos, games, and group chats with friends at my fingertips—I would likely have acted the same way.

Even though the only community I knew growing up has changed, the need communities serve is still present—common good, security, and enjoyment.

Our planet is something we all share, a common good.

Preservation of it should be a common goal.

As I think again of the boat on the water and who's in it, I know it is steered by connectivity and community toward sustainability. This knowledge can help us get into our own boats. Individuals benefit from being part of a community. Communities grow stronger through individual actions. Would that be enough to begin a sustainability journey?

As I turned my boat and attention north of the village, the answer was obvious. Dark clouds were gathering. They were there when I was a boy, and they were likely there even before I was born in 1970. My experience growing up in Nassau was of community and connectivity in abundance. If those things alone were enough to combat the forces fighting against sustainability—the things that can drive us to do things that may hurt others for our own gain—the dark clouds would have never formed.

But they did.

It was time to ride into the storm that had been brewing for 60 years instead of passively riding it out on the sideline.

Chapter 3

STAY OUT OF THE LAKE

John Muir's three-day trip in 1903 with then President Theodore Roosevelt could be considered the most significant camping trip in conservation history. John Muir was a naturalist, writer, staunch advocate for forests, and founder of the Sierra Club. They camped amongst the giant sequoias in Mariposa Grove, were photographed atop Glacier Point, and visited the Yosemite Valley floor.[11]

In simple terms, Muir was more of a preservationist—his ideal was to protect nature from use. His aim was to permit little to no industrial profit from federal lands.

Roosevelt, on the other hand, was more of a conservationist—his philosophy was one that allowed the proper use of nature. In Roosevelt's interpretation, land owned by the federal government could be used for recreation by the public and could also be used for industrial endeavors and research if done responsibly.

Muir had a big impact on Roosevelt. Upon his return to

Washington, the president made a series of decisions that seemingly stemmed at least in part from his trip with Muir.

During his administration, the National Park System expanded substantially. He established five national parks and paved the way for many more in the years after he left office. During his tenure, in 1906 he signed the Act of Preservation of American Antiquities—the first United States law to provide general protection for any general kind of cultural or natural resource—and designated 18 national monuments. He was also the first president to create a Federal Bird Reserve and would establish 51 of these during his administration. These reserves would later become modern day national wildlife refuges. Today, there are national wildlife refuges in every state. Overall, Roosevelt protected about 230 million acres of public land.[12]

Today, the National Park Service (NPS) oversees 63 national parks and many more monuments, military sites, historic sites, seashores, rivers, and trails covering 84 million acres. The agency is focused on preserving natural and cultural values and manages resources of the land for the enjoyment and inspiration of future generations.

Alongside the NPS, the USDA Forest manages 193 million acres: 155 National Forests, 20 National Grasslands, 1 National Tallgrass Prairie. Its job is to sustain the health, diversity, and productivity of national forests. National forests are managed for more purposes than national parks—timber, wildlife, recreation, grazing, fishing, etc.

So, why do we have both national parks and national forests?

National parks have more a preservationist view, just like Muir advocated for. Meanwhile, national forests lean more toward conservationism, and align with Roosevelt's vision.[13]

That singular camping event was instrumental in setting America on a path of preservation and conservation to meet the needs of generations, today and in the future.

In 2018, my family and I visited the same places that Muir and Roosevelt did 115 years ago. The towering sequoias, beautiful vistas atop million-year-old rock formations, and beauty of the valley floor was seemingly as it was back then.

The parks we enjoy today depended on that Roosevelt–Muir trip and the path forged thereafter.

The people involved with Nassau Lake were subject to a very different path.

Nassau Lake sits about 2 miles north of the traffic light at the center of town, on the outskirts of the village. It covers 174 acres and feeds streams and other lakes in the area. A dam holds back water at the southern tip of the lake.

My parents mostly let us do anything we wanted in the village as kids, save for one unbreakable rule: we knew never to go in the lake.

We would sometimes ride our bikes there—to us it was a place of intrigue. Houses nestled along the tree-lined perimeter and sunlight reflected off the water. The wide oval shape of the lake allowed for almost a full panoramic view from most shoreline vantage points. A beautiful scene, certainly, but no lake activity.

A seasonal outdoor burger joint would be a dinner destination for our family more than a few times each summer. It was fun to sit lakeside and eat all together. Our only interaction with the lake was skipping stones across its surface. But we never went in.

I rarely if ever saw any boats on it. As a kid, I did not understand why, I just knew it was off limits.

In middle school and high school my school bus route followed the road that skirted the lake. Each morning and afternoon, the bus would make multiple stops along the lakefront to board or drop off students. One such stop was in front of a green cement building at the southern end of the lake. The abandoned one-story building was dated to the point that it was hard to tell what purpose it had served in its prime.

The letters "arin" were just about legible from the bus window but I didn't try to figure out what that meant. I had my own struggles of trying to survive middle and high school.

Little did I know it was my first clue to the secrets of the lake.

Nassau Lake is actually a reservoir. Lakes are natural, whereas reservoirs are not. When a dam is built on a large stream or river, water builds up behind it creating a man-made body of water. Jonathan Hoag, who settled in Nassau in 1792, built the dam, and in doing so flooded the surrounding meadow and swampland which served as a natural basin to create a large head of water. He called it Hoag's Pond, which was later re-named Nassau Lake.

The Valatie Kill stream feeds Nassau Lake from the north and continues out the southern end once the water flows over the dam. It then flows for 2 miles to form the western edge of the village of Nassau and continues south approximately 20 miles through Kinderhook Lake, Kinderhook Creek, and Stockport Creek to finally empty into the Hudson River.

Prior to Hoag and the European Henry Hudson's arrival in 1609 when his ship the *Half Moon* arrived less than 10 miles from

Nassau, the Stockbridge and Munsee Native American tribes of the Mohican nation roamed the swath of land east of the Hudson River. They extended to present day Vermont and New Hampshire and from Manhattan Island to Lake Champlain. The two tribes were similar and are often referred to as the Stockbridge–Munsee community.

The Stockbridge–Munsee always lived with nature. As the seasons changed, so did the activities of the people. Springtime was peak for fishing, planting, and gathering syrup from maple trees. Summer and fall were for harvesting the plantings from spring and for hunting. The Stockbridge–Munsee used every part of the animals they killed and always thanked the creator for their bounty. Hunting remained a high priority in the winter along with weaving clothing and blankets, carving, and repairing eating utensils and weapons.

"Every eight to ten years villages would move so that the land could replenish itself." The Stockbridge–Munsee often built their homes near rivers and streams. The stream that Hoag later chose to build a dam on to create Nassau Lake also fit the description of a village site for the Stockbridge–Munsee people.[14]

The new European settlers believed that individuals had the right to own land and establish permanent settlements. Self-ownership leads to self-action to act in ways that may solely benefit the individual who owns the land to the potential detriment of the community at large. Individual land ownership promoted pure survival of the owner. Land that was not owned by the individual was also less a priority. In an ownership model, land with no proprietor has an increased potential of being less respected, less sacred, less preserved.

Conversely, Native Americans generally did not "appreciate

the idea of land as a commodity, especially not in terms of individual ownership." Land was a common good like water, air, or sunlight. They believed it was sacred and should be treated with respect. Land preservation, therefore, allowed for long-term survival.[15] European settlers' ownership philosophy along with their new culture and the introduction of new diseases ultimately combined to push the Stockbridge–Munsee people off the land, reduce the population, and erode the culture over the course of many years.

The fundamental idea of land as a common good to preserve as a high priority has been de-emphasized and, in many ways, lost. The right to ownership has become engrained in our society—the right to own land, a home, a car. The desire to own seems to be one deterrent to getting into a sustainability boat.

Hoag built mills downstream from the dam. The water from the lake was sluiced down the wide stream to provide a source of power. The mills could run from the waters of Nassau Lake for as long as there was a supply. "On busy days, it might have been common for the mills to run the lake nearly empty."[16]

The mills sat on the banks of the rushing water on the northern end of the village near the corner of Elm Street and Lake Avenue. Some of the buildings have been taken down while others have changed hands, purpose, and appearance. From the sidewalk in front of my house as a youth, about a half-block down to the north sat one of the historic mills. An 1895 photo found in the Nassau Library shows the building with the name NASSAU MILLS in bold capital letters painted on the side. The photograph had the caption "Grist mill at Lake Avenue and Elm Street established in 1792".[17] In the 1980s it housed a small pen factory.

My parents live in the same house on Elm Street to this day.

The view is the same. The building is still there, although now dilapidated. The water still flows.

Hoag's mills were followed by a hotel and stores built in and around the village a mile south of the newly formed lake. The young town began to attract a wide array of visitors. Gilbert du Motier, Marquis de Lafayette of Revolutionary War fame and Joseph Bonaparte, older brother of Napoleon and King of Spain, spent portions of several summers in the hotel in the early 1800s. United States generals John B. Wool and Alexander Macomb, along with the eighth president of the United States, Martin Van Buren, were also "frequent patrons" of the town.[18]

The lake's visibility as a destination grew as a result of a newly formed railway system that ran tangent to the southern tip of the lake. In 1899, the Albany and Hudson Electric Railway was finished—37 miles in length and at the time only the third inter-urban line in the United States. The train connected 14 villages from Albany to Hudson with over 30 stops. The track ran mostly east 15 miles to Nassau before bending south. It was an approximate two-hour trip one way and provided easy transport for shopping, entertainment, and work. At its peak, the railway system moved over 1,000,000 people a year.

A hydropower plant at Stuyvesant Falls toward the southern end of the rail line provided all the electricity needed to run the trains. The 1899 railway had it right—local waterpower that was carbon free. Ironically, our goal today is to reduce our reliance on fossil fuels and reduce carbon emissions.[19]

The railway was instrumental in the lake attracting restaurants, hotels, and interested landowners over the next 50-plus years. In the post-World War I years, "summer colonies" sprang up on the northern tip, where Albany residents viewed the lake and cottages as an exclusive summer location. In the 1920s, *The Albany Evening News* and *Knickerbocker Press* developed a plan to sell over 1,000 small lots. The vision of Nassau Lake Park as a summer resort was born. Nassau Lake would be advertised as a place to have fun.

On Thursday May 8, 1924, *The Berkshire Evening Eagle* based out of Pittsfield, MA, fifteen miles to the east, ran an article touting Nassau Lake. "Nassau Lake Park is an ideal place to send your family for the summer and must soon be a leading summer resort for the people from Albany and other nearby cities."[20]

The railway system's popularity began to decline when the automobile began its ascension as the dominant form of transportation. By 1930, the railway was bankrupt. However, interest in the lake as a destination never wavered.

"Albany Boy Saved From Drowning in Nassau Lake" was the headline in *The Times Record* on August 14, 1946. The boy was saved by two local fishermen. The last two sentences of the article offer a glimpse of how the lake was still viewed in the mid-1940s.

"The Flynn family had left Albany Saturday for a *two-week vacation* [my emphasis] at the lake. Their cottage was near the dock from which the boy fell."[21]

The 1952 telephone book listed 11 restaurants/taverns, seven of which were located adjacent to the lake. Angler's Rest, Lakeview Manor, Mantica's, and The Nassau Lake Clubhouse dotted the eastern side, while Capron's, Wappler's Lakewood Inn, the Aldrich Hotel, the Morey Park Tavern, the Harris Inn, and the Nassau Lake Hotel covered the western and northern sides.[22]

The 1957 second annual Nassau Little League program provided more evidence of what life was like on the lake prior to the

1960s. I found an original copy in the Nassau Public Library archives. Advertisements for local businesses supporting the new youth organization appeared in the black and white 20-plus page booklet.

Mantica's Italian Restaurant
Hot Pizza, Italian Food Cooked to Order, Clams
East Side of Nassau Lake
Phone 8-2532 or 8-1461

Angler's Rest
Nassau Lake

Harris Inn
Choice Food and Refreshments
Nassau Lake

Kenyon's Restaurant
Picnic Grounds and Swimming
Morey Park, Nassau Lake
Phone 8-3539

Star Boat Livery
Boats for Hire - For Sale - Built and Repaired
Bait for Sale
Nassau Lake, West Side
Phone 8-3912

Lakeside Inn
Choice Food and Refreshments
West Side, Nassau Lake
Phone 8-3646

Food, boats, bait, swimming, fishing, picnics, lake activity, relaxation, and fun.

Described by some as a "Little Lake George," Nassau Lake

seemed poised to continue to build on its foundation. Lake George is a 32-mile-long freshwater lake in the Adirondack Mountains. Just 90 minutes north of Nassau, it remains to this day a summer destination for vacationers. In 2016, Lake George was listed as one of the top 10 cleanest freshwater lakes in the United States.

The wholesome and picturesque reality of Nassau Lake prior to the 1960s was never seen by my generation. The rule "stay out of the lake" was never questioned. For me, "stay out" turned into "avoid" and was eventually cemented into "ignore."

What changed?

I began to find answers as I looked back to the 1950s.

From 1952 to 1968, hazardous substances including volatile organic compounds and polychlorinated biphenyls (PCBs) were dumped in a nearby landfill. They seeped into the groundwater and infected the lake 2 miles southwest of the dump site. Winding streams and underwater aquifers acted as bobsled runs for the chemicals to move downhill. The finish line was Nassau Lake. The chemicals still lie at the bottom today.

The days of swimming, boating, fishing, eating lakeside, and investment were over. The realization of what was happening took years to take full effect although the consequences could be traced back to this singular path-dependent event.

PATH DEPENDENCE

Path dependence is a concept found in social sciences and economics. The idea is essentially that the outcome of something is dependent on the path of previous outcomes, rather than simply on current conditions. History matters and drives the outcomes of today.

While changing current conditions may be possible, the cost and time to do so can be prohibitive. Path dependence is often caused by either a single event in time or a long-term process that gains consensus and thus becomes hard to change.

Fossil fuel, solar, and wind power have each been used in society for hundreds (wind and solar for thousands) of years. The development of each for widespread power use differs, but as it happened solar and wind were beaten to the mass power generation finish line. The invention of the steam engine powered by coal drove the Industrial Revolution in the late 1700s and 1800s while technological advances to harness wind and solar lagged: the first United States utility-scale wind turbines were only developed in the 1970s[23] and Bell Labs produced the first modern solar panels in 1954.[24]

As fossil fuel use exploded so did the release of carbon into the atmosphere. At the start of the Industrial Revolution in 1750, 280 parts per million (ppm) of carbon dioxide were present in the atmosphere. Today, that number is approximately 415 ppm.[25] Approximately 65% of human-produced greenhouse gas emissions comes from the fossil fuels used to power our society.[26]

Sequestered carbon in the form of oil, coal, and natural gas underground were given a one-way vertical ticket to the atmosphere freeway. The freeway has been accepting carbon dioxide as a by-product of burning fossil fuels for over 200 years to the extent that there is now a log jam of trapped carbon absorbing the heat reflecting off the Earth's surface. With no means of expanding the freeway and no off ramps, the log jam moves toward gridlock. Gridlock in the form of increased trapped heat.

The steam engine, then, is a path-dependent event. It began a 250-year-plus tsunami of power creation all dependent on burning carbon.

Muir and Roosevelt's three-day camping trip in 1903 was an event that set a path to increased conservation and preservation. Over time since then, setting land aside for national parks and protected areas became the norm, making conservation regulations hard to change, and creating an altogether different path-dependent event.

But, in the early 1950s when a decision was made to transport toxic waste out of the nearby cities of Albany and Schenectady to a dumping site in Nassau, the lake and surrounding area were forced to move away from conservation and preservation and became path dependent to that event. At the time, the environment was not a serious stakeholder at the business gaming table. The players either did not know the long-term effects of dumping waste in the environment or were uninterested in knowing—they simply needed a dumping ground. Over the course of 16 years the chemical waste, transported in 55-gallon barrels, formed a lagoon of toxicity and a barrel junkyard. The waste was dumped in open pits, unusable drums were either left on the perimeter or buried, and chemicals were burned. Toxic chemicals escaped, seeped into groundwater, and flowed into tributaries. The effects are both long-lasting and devastating.

What I experienced as a boy was what seemed to be a dead lake: no activity and seemingly no intention to undo what had been done. What I experienced was 60 years and three generations of a lake on hospice and a surrounding community impacted by confounding loss and destruction.

One day. One event. One decision that was repeated over and over.

Path dependence is a valuable tool in building knowledge and fighting for the health of our community and planet. At minimum, it provides awareness of what decisions can evolve into. At best, it forces decisions to be well thought out amongst multiple stakeholders.

Chapter 4

TOXIC INSPIRATION

The effects went well beyond the lake itself. I needed to conduct research and talk to more people to understand the full impact. In January of 2021, I visited the landfill near Nassau Lake for the first time—69 years had passed since the first chemicals were dumped. Maybe going to the site would provide perspective and motivation to do something.

On a 5°F evening in the dead of winter, I re-routed my car to the eastern side of the lake as I took an alternate route home from my parents' house. The road leads away from the lake after nearly touching it at the southern end. After a five-minute ride, I came upon the road on the right that led to the dump site. I took the turn.

The pavement turned to dirt and as the road narrowed, I instinctively slowed down. The road snaked through barren trees asleep for the winter. It was bitterly cold and the sky a lifeless gray. The leafless branches hung over the road reaching down toward my car with skeleton fingers. The gradient grew steeper. The loneliness of the road seeped into my car. I made sure the windows were rolled up and the doors were locked.

I began to see posted signs to keep out and wire fencing signaling the same. As I rose in elevation, so did my nerves and anticipation of what was ahead. I drove up to the high point of the hill. To the right was what seemed to be the entrance to the landfill, long since closed, and a small, seemingly deserted hut. I stopped the car but did not get out. I looked all around to see if anyone was watching me, a voice in my head grappling with an encounter that was likely never to come. I was preparing to answer the question, "What are you doing here?"

The wire barriers, signage, cold, dirt road, and abandoned shed all combined to make the stillness of my surroundings weigh down on me like a mounting sadness. The stillness evoked a familiar feeling—the same one I had when looking at the lake itself. The silence from the dump site had slowly spread to silence the lake too. I turned the car around and headed back down the track to find pavement.

As I drove, I tried to envision what it had been like in 1952 when that first truck full of waste pulled onto the dirt road. Did they know what would happen as a result? Was it a purposeful and devious act or just business? Was it illegal at the time?

"Please Don't Eat Those Fish" was the headline on July 7, 1988 in the *Chatham Courier*. I found the actual paper in the archives of the Nassau Public Library. The small village library's high ceilings and stacks of unique books and periodicals spoke to its charm. The old wooden floors still creaked, and the glorious scent of old books filled the air—an entire history of a community sat on the shelves. The overtly friendly staff combined with the old building to make a stranger who had been away for a long time feel welcome.

Finding an article related to my search from the same paper I delivered as a boy strengthened my resolve and motivation. The front-page story stated that Nassau Lake was given an "Eat None" recommendation from the New York State Department of Health. The Department's new advisory for sport fishing revised the recommended restrictions on the consumption of fish from the freshwater lake as the result of recent sampling. PCBs can bioaccumulate in living organisms over time and thus enter the food chain to biomagnify the effect.

The article went on to say that over five different fish species all had PCB levels exceeding the federal limit of 2ppm (parts per million), an increase compared to samplings from previous years. PCBs are classified by the EPA as probable human carcinogens and can have negative effects on reproductive, endocrine, neurological, and immune systems.[27]

The dumping from decades prior had invaded the lake and affected the surrounding community. Over 70 years since, the chemicals were still working like toxic thieves, slowly stealing businesses, crushing investment, decreasing home values, infecting wildlife, posing health risks, and killing summer activity.

As I'd looked out over the old dump site before driving away, I thought of Occam's Razor.

William of Ockham was a philosopher in the early 1300s. He embraced a "keep it simple" concept as a standard guideline for thinking through issues logically. Occam is a misspelling of his real name. The term "Razor" denotes the cutting away of unnecessary information or cluttering thoughts. The thinking suggests that complex explanations are less likely to be true than simpler ones. Instead of piecing together a sequence of unlikely events, take a step back and look for the reasoning with the fewest moving variables.

For example, when I have an onset of chest pain, do I think I am having a heart attack as a healthy 50-year-old, or do I think something I did a few days before, like lifting weights, may have caused a slight chest muscle strain? Occam's Razor would signal the muscle strain as the simpler and more likely explanation.

In terms of Nassau Lake, Occam's Razor directed my thoughts to the waste being dumped in secret. Unwanted, unusable chemicals transported and dumped in a seemingly unknown place. Unscrupulous actors coordinated the clandestine actions. That seemed like the simple explanation.

But before I could fully accept Occam's principal result, I had to know more. I had a lot to research and understand. Who were the actors at play? How was conservation viewed in the mid-20th century? How could dumping chemicals in this way possibly have seemed acceptable? What was life like in the mid-20th century when this first began?

All these questions were founded in the image that began this journey of the girl water skiing and the truck carrying those barrels.

In stark contrast is Burden Lake, 7 miles from Nassau Lake which, on a summer day, is bursting with activity.

I have visited Burden Lake many times. I know people with summer homes on the lake as well as full-time residents. I eat at Kay's Pizza which sits on the water's edge, a wildly popular restaurant that has been there for over 60 years. I have boated on Burden Lake and watched people pull fish out of the lake for years.

The only difference between the two lakes is location. Burden

Lake sits north of the landfill. Nassau Lake sits to the south. The landfill splits the difference.

Groundwater flows southwest of the landfill affecting waterways and lakes downstream of it. The dam at the end of Nassau Lake serves as a barrier to most chemicals escaping. Nassau Lake became, in effect, a sacrificial lamb, holding the chemicals the best it could while the streams and bodies of water to the north never experienced the catastrophe.

Burden Lake was entirely unaffected. The impacts of pollution are inequitable.

Pollution is a disease with no cure, it can only be prevented. So, how can we prevent it?

In part, by embracing a circular economy, and circular thinking and processes, which stand in direct contrast to the more dominant, throwaway economy we live in today. This predominant linear system takes resources, makes products, and disposes of waste in a landfill or incineration.

But a circular economy bends the linear line to eliminate waste. The by-products of one process become a feedstock for the next. Returning bottles to the store for 5 cents is an example of circularity. The aluminum can, glass, or plastic bottles dropped off are sold to processors and manufacturers who in turn use the material to make another product.

In nature, when things die, their remains become part of the soil, water, or air to enable other things to grow. Nature has no landfills or incineration plants for waste. Everything is a resource.

If the circular economy had been in full implementation in the 1950s, toxic by-products would not exist as the process itself would produce only nontoxic by-products. Ideally, just as in nature, there is no waste in circular economic models. At the very least non-circular by-products—those which have no current circular alternatives—should be viewed as such and therefore treated as such upon use.

Closing the loop for an item like plastic bottles in a deposit drop-off can take a circular path to ideally making another bottle but can also be used to make other items such as clothes. Clothing companies like Patagonia sell shirts using recycled polyester. A circular economy embraces all the steps—gathering materials at the end of life, sorting the materials, making a new product, and then marketing and selling the item.

Adoption of circular principles is forward-thinking and helps prevent inadvertent poor path-dependent decisions.

Nassau Lake is 1.5 miles from the house I grew up in. I must have passed the lake over 5,000 times in my life. It was on my bus route, on my drive to school, and is the same route I take when I go to my parents' house from our current house 12 miles north. It is part of my tapestry.

But despite this, for years I was blinded by my own selfish survival instinct. The one that says if it's not in my backyard, then it's not my problem. Even though it is in my backyard, I had been ignoring it. As I looked to accumulate reasons to get into the boat, all I had managed to do was stumble upon a reason not to—selfishness. I had ignored for 50 years what was not in my immediate self-interest.

It was time to get to know the lake. Time to experience its story and to understand more. Time to stop analogizing about my fictitious boat and get into a real one, to spend time with a sick friend in need of being heard and helped.

Chapter 5

OBSERVATIONS

Donald P. Sutherland Elementary School sits atop a hill in the village of Nassau. The front doors of the red-brick building are guarded by tall, white columns and a flagpole is centered in a large, finely groomed lawn in direct line with the front doors. The school's stately appearance was matched by the care and great memories I have from my kindergarten through 4th grade education years. Mrs. Ward, Mrs. Chapman, Mrs. Singleton, Mrs. Donahue, Mrs. Krebs, Mr. Evans, and Mr. Citrolo were my original guides to education.

In the back of the school is a nature trail. A short path that winds through the woods mostly running parallel to a stream. The stream originates 3 miles north in Nassau Lake with the dump site a few miles further up. Water falls over the dam that corks Nassau Lake and into the Valatie Kill waterway. The 10- to 30-foot-wide stream meanders south to run tangent to the western side of the village and behind the elementary school. From age four to eight my teachers would take us out to the trail as a part of our educational experience.

The idea was for us to enjoy being outside and to be on alert to what was happening all around us. I recall the teachers asking us to "observe" as we walked along the trail. When we got back to the classroom, we would list what we saw. While I think I was more excited to be outside at the time, being a keen observer as a child set the foundation for my need to question why and how today.

Forty-five years after my elementary school days and six months after visiting the dump site for the first time, I wandered back to the trail behind the school. The Valatie Kill still flows as it always has but lesson plans had clearly changed since my youth as evidenced by the overgrown trail, untrampled and unexplored by elementary school students. But I wasn't done learning. My lake lessons were about to begin.

As I secured the kayak in the back of the truck, an experience I had avoided for so long was now something I could not wait to have. My anticipation reinforced the thought that the trip may be less about learning something new than about approaching an old experience, about seeing the lake in a different way.

As I drove, the rule "stay out of the lake" echoed in my head. I didn't recall ever having touched the water. A mantra beaten into me for so long had created an unfounded fear of the effects of exposure to the chemicals. Fear without information, paralyzing action, and likely contributing to a false narrative nudged my memory to the way people reacted to AIDS in the 1980s.

Acquired Immune Deficiency Syndrome (AIDS) grabbed international attention in the early 1980s. Information about the disease was scarce in the earliest days, which led to uninformed attitudes toward people with AIDS. In 1986, 44% of Americans reported that they or someone they knew avoided places where homosexuals might be present as a precaution to avoid contracting the virus. A poll revealed that 60% of Americans agreed that people with AIDS should be made to carry a card declaring they had the virus and 21% of Americans said people with AIDS should be isolated from the rest of society.[28]

I was a teenager in the mid-1980s and remember feeling uninformed and, to some degree, fearful. I followed a public narrative, which seems selfishly safe to me now. Uninformed, fearful, selfishly safe—these three impediments tie the bow on how I packaged attitudes to Nassau Lake. It was time to get informed, to know for certain if the fear was justified, and to help find some answers to a problem bigger than me.

I arrived at the lake at 11:00 a.m. on a warm late spring morning. The bright sun on a brilliant blue backdrop a stark contrast to the gray, listless sky from my landfill visit five months prior. I took my socks and shoes off and approached the bank. I was alone. I dragged my kayak to the water's edge, paused, and heard echoes from my parents, newspaper articles, notices, and the voice of public opinion ringing in my head. Embarrassment from feeding the echoes for so long combined with an eagerness to finally have this experience propelled me to lift my bare foot off the ground and step forward into the lake. Done. I quickly hopped into my kayak and did not think again about the echoes.

I had two goals that day. One was to smash through the "stay out of the lake" mantra baked into my being. Mission accomplished. Second was to try to see the things I had read about, that people had told me about, and that I had thought about for years: remnants of Nassau Lake being a summer destination in the early half of the 1900s; remains of the restaurants and marina that used to form a ring around the lake; the dam originally built centuries prior by Jonathan Hoag; the inlets of water that carried the chemicals. Mostly, I wanted to see if there was any activity on the lake and whether, although I knew better, I could actually see the chemicals in shallow water. If I could actually see the chemicals, I thought, it would serve as confirmation of what I already knew.

For the next two and a half hours, I paddled in my kayak first hugging the shoreline and finally venturing to the middle of the lake where the girl crouched on her skis 70 years before.

Small cottages and other visually coveted waterfront properties capped the northern end of the lake. Many had been constructed in the early 1900s, and each property had its own space with open lake views.

The northern side is where the Valatie Kill stream joins the lake, transporting the toxic chemicals from the dump site a few miles away. The water was clear at the entry point but I knew that the muddy bottom, just 3 feet below me, was the bandage that concealed the lake's sores. This was the spot where gravity steps in, where the flowing water drops off its chemical cargo with no gondola ride available to go back up the hill.

Along the longer eastern side, more homes lined the shoreline. In the background, rolling, round-top hills framed the view, creating an image of interlocking frowns as the landscape gently snaked up and down. The green hills stood in vibrant contrast to the blue sky above.

At the very southern tip, a dam about 50 feet wide is a barrier for the water to climb. When the lake is full, water gushes over the top of the dam and re-forms into the Valatie Kill stream. Otherwise, the dam would act as a permanent hold on its contents.

The stream flowing south of the lake runs through the village of Nassau, behind the elementary school, and then on to a string of neighboring communities, eventually emptying into Kinderhook Lake 15 miles downstream.

The lake, therefore, was a bathtub with no drain. The spigots for incoming water were north of the dam. The water could only exit the lake when the "tub" overflowed the walls at the southern end. With no drain in the lake, chemicals in the water sank to the bottom to take up permanent residence.

Along the final edge of the lake was a two-lane road gating the lake on the west side which ran mostly parallel to the lake's length. It was the side I had traveled so many times with little thought to the body of water next to me. The road was the main thoroughfare that connected the neighboring towns.

On the whole, I saw very few boat docks that day. There were no floating island swimming docks in the entire lake. The lack of docks signaled a lack of activity. The restaurants I had read about that once surrounded the lake were all gone but for one. Most of the restaurant buildings I'd seen in old photographs were wiped clean from my current view. Confirmation of their existence was now confined to books in the local library and reminiscing with older residents.

Being on the lake for the first time reinforced what I already knew. The effect of the chemicals had diminished activity and development on and around the lake. Observing this from a new perspective brought me closer to understanding the ripple effects beyond what I could see.

Remember the green cement building with "arin" on the side I used to see out of the school bus window in the 1980s? I could see it from my kayak conveniently located in a small inlet in the southwest corner just 20 to 30 yards from the water's edge. It was still standing but now no letters remained to decode. My curiosity about that building led me to Kurt Vincent, who helped me see that my boyhood bus window view offered a window to the past.

Kurt is a longtime resident, active community member, and historian of Nassau. His book *Images of America: Nassau* documents the history of Nassau through old pictures that somehow survived decades, some even centuries. Local stories handed down from generation to generation and all tied together with Kurt's seasoned narration.

I met Kurt on a brilliant blue-sky fall afternoon. We sat on benches with a beautiful view of the lake from the southern end— the same place the railway stopped many years ago. Kurt told me about the history of Nassau and described what the place would have been like 100 years ago with the train system pumping people through its railway veins, connecting them to the array of towns along the way.

I pointed to the now beige building and asked Kurt what it used to be 70 years ago.

"A marina," he said.

Long gone. The marina had long since shut down. Weathering had already faded out the "M" and the "a" on the green concrete by the time I was 12. The water activities that marinas represent were now abandoned just like the building itself.

SEEING IS BELIEVING

I did not see the chemicals on my trip to the lake but I found someone who had seen them. Don Strevell Jr. grew up in Nassau. As of this writing, he is 81 years old. A boy in the 1940s and a teen in the late 1950s, he knew Nassau before, during, and after the chemical dumping. He served in the military after high school and settled in a neighboring town to raise his family. Don is a straightforward, meticulous to detail, and highly respected man. I reached out to chat about his memories.

Not only did he walk the same streets I did as a boy, but he also grew up in the same house I did. Don is my uncle.

"I remember seeing the truck," Don told me. "It was a rack truck with barrels loaded on the back." I imagined a small cab in front for the driver and an open-air flatbed back for cargo—six to eight barrels standing vertically and held in by short side walls and maybe some strapping.

"The Gulf gas station at the corner of Malden and Church Street," he said, looking at me as if I knew where the station had been. "The driver would fill up there. The letters 'GE' were written on some of the barrels. They smelled."

"Smelled?" I repeated.

"Like chemicals," Don said without hesitation.

"With the company name on the barrels, a noticeable chemical smell, and a truck filling up at the local gas station and moving through the village like a regular commuter, it doesn't sound like the truck was hiding what it was doing," I said.

"No, it was just part of everyday life. No one knew. How could we have known?" he replied.

By 1970, the truck carrying its barrels over many years and many trips had helped fill the dumpsite. It became a chemical lagoon devoid of plant and animal life. Shortly thereafter, the dumping ground was covered over with soil and converted to a landfill.[29]

The Dewey Loeffel Landfill profile page on the EPA website states, "The site was used as a dump for hazardous waste generated by several companies including General Electric (GE), Bendix Corporation (now Honeywell), and Schenectady Chemicals (now SI Group)."[30]

The hazardous waste dumping a few miles from Nassau Lake occurred prior to the formation of the Environmental Protection Agency in 1970. So, without a governing body in charge, who—if anyone—was regulating disposal?

Was the toxic dumping deliberate? Unintentional? Both?

When did the companies generating the waste, the people transporting the waste, and the company receiving the waste know that dumping in open pits would cause catastrophic environmental damage? More importantly, once they knew, when did they act?

DUMPING NOW

When did we know that releasing carbon dioxide into the atmosphere would cause such damage? In 1895, Swedish chemist Svante Arrhenius calculated that if CO_2 levels doubled, global temperatures could increase by 5°C. Over a century later, climate modeling is finding his numbers were not that far off.[31]

But we have yet to act to significantly enough to curb carbon emissions. Since 1970, CO_2 emissions have increased by about 90%.[32]

What can any of us do?

Cycling instead of driving, buying second-hand or repurposing clothing, fixing a tool instead of buying new, recycling plastic water bottles, composting grass trimmings, and collecting rainwater in a water butt are small yet positive steps we can all take. They save resources, lower emissions, and can subtly provide a boost to the psyche. If done consistently, collectively, and cross-culturally, actions like these can change instincts from self-preservation to long-term Earth preservation.

Yet, unfortunately, these seemingly small individual actions can also quickly feel inconsequential with every Intergovernmental Panel on Climate Change (IPCC) data report.

The IPCC was formed in 1988 by the World Meteorological Organization and the United Nations Environment Programme, and is the leading scientific organizational body related to climate change research. Its purpose is to provide scientific assessment of climate change on an ongoing basis including its impacts and future risks and options for adaptation and mitigation.

"Climate change widespread, rapid, and intensifying—IPCC"[33] was the headline from the August 2021 report.

Among a wide range of findings in the report, two in particular caught my attention.

1. The last decade was hotter than any period in the last 125,000 years.

2. Science can now link specific weather events to human-made climate change.

Both factors are the result of large increases of carbon dioxide in the atmosphere.

The report also states that since 1970, global surface temperatures have risen faster than in any other 50-year period over the past 2,000 years. I was born in 1970. This issue spans my lifetime.

It makes me think I have something to do with it.

Toxic chemicals dumped 60 years ago in a landfill changed Nassau Lake. Dumping CO_2 into the atmosphere is causing and will continue to cause catastrophic effects.

Dumping then. Dumping now.

Science-based data cited in the IPCC report surrounding how we interact with the environment is overwhelming. The magnitude of the problems can sap hope and enthusiasm to act—another reason not to get into the boat. I realized that if I hope to help people find their own boat and begin to move, I must offer suggestions for change that do not seem irrelevant or fruitless given the enormity of the problem.

I have been in the plastic bag manufacturing business for 30 years. I am very familiar with packaging, alternatives, their values, and their end-of-life options. We have been filling recycling bins and trash bins for years. Analyzing what we were putting in them became appealing. I decided to start there.

Chapter 6

SORTED

confess that at first, I had to fight the urge to inaction, to ignore the problem. I tried not to focus on overcoming the enormity of it all. Instead, I concentrated on what I could—I narrowed my focus to my household and my family's consumption within the household. Over 20% of all United Sates emissions are directly attributed to household consumption.[34]

Thanks to my full immersion in the circular economy, I began to think of all by-products more as resources, and less as waste. After all, in a perfect circular economy, there is no waste. By-products from one process become feedstock for another—all waste is captured at the end of life, then reprocessed or composted and made into a new product to be marketed and sold. The material loops are closed. Closed-loop systems see everything as a potential resource and eliminate the idea of waste to landfill or worse, dumping it into the natural environment. Arguably, circularity for some chemicals and products is a challenge with no current viable alternatives but circularity for household waste seemed more attainable.

The benefits of closed loops for materials include reducing the amount of waste sent to landfills, conserving use of finite raw materials, saving energy, and lowering carbon emissions' impact on global warming. Using existing materials as building blocks for new items is a win on multiple levels but collecting and sorting them poses the first set of challenges.

Plastic bottles, small wrappers, paper cup holders, paper bags, metal cans, plastic food packaging, plastic bags, and much more are everyday escapees from the waste management system. Infrastructure gaps, limited consumer education, general apathy toward proper disposal, businesses' general lack of interest in the process, unclear labeling on how to dispose of the package, limited value of waste, and lack of government support for circular policies results in a less than perfect system.

That system results in low overall recycle rates, very low composting participation, high landfill-bound waste, and leakage of waste in the natural environment. I wanted to fill those holes, ditch the malaise, and drill down on each package to see if our family could achieve a circular economy for our waste—at least for a week.

WASTE WEEK

Waste week occurred within my household in June 2022, driven by three statistics from the EPA:

1. Americans produce 4.9 lbs of waste per day

2. 32% of waste is recycled or composted[35]

3. 75% of Americans' waste stream is recyclable[36]

We are a family of five—my wife and I are 51 years old, and our three sons are age 19, 17, and 12. For one week, we inventoried all our waste by general material type, weight, and end-of-life options available in our current infrastructure. The goal of the week was two-fold:

First, with additional efforts to sort waste, *how much could we improve on each statistic?* I assumed these three goals were averages for Americans who were not necessarily trying like we would be to divert anything we could away from landfill. With added awareness, could we achieve less than 4.9 lbs of waste per person? If we really tried to recycle or compost everything, how much higher would the percentage be above 32%? Would we be able to recycle more than 75% of our waste?

Second, I wanted to see *how close we could get to the aspirational zero waste.* This is the goal of a circular economy within the current waste disposal streams available. The zero waste ethos forces us to view items as a resource, with each of us being solely responsible for giving the item the chance for another life.

Disposal decisions have two paths: end the life or begin a new one. To keep materials out of landfill and out of the natural environment, I had to first figure out what I was going to do with the household waste as I sorted it. In my municipality there are only four options:

1. <u>Recycle</u>. Curbside in a single-stream bin or, for plastic bags, return them to the in-store drop-off bin. The material's new life comes in the form of recycling centers bailing like items to be sold as a feedstock for a new product.

2. <u>Compost</u>. Our family bought a Lomi—a small composting countertop unit for food scraps and other organic waste. About the size of a small microwave, Lomi

accelerates the composting process from months to hours. The organic scraps' new life comes in the form of compost to grow new things.

3. <u>Reuse</u>. Does this item need to be disposed of? If not, the existing material or product life continues.

4. <u>Landfill</u>. This ends the life of the material.

Each night, I gathered up all our waste for the day to log the weight and description of the waste. My "laboratory" was the garage. An old card table served as my desk. The compost unit and small weighing scale absorbed half the workspace leaving just enough room for documenting results. A recycle bin, a landfill bin, a plastic bag bin, a compost bowl, and a reuse bin surrounded the card table. A small radio kept me company in the 45–60-minute nightly exercise.

The process was oddly familiar. I was alone shuffling through different items to put them in the right place just as I had years ago albeit with a different medium—the sorting, valuing, and statistical aspect reminded me of my youth and love of baseball cards.

My best friend Tom and I would frequent local stores for their penny candy but mostly for their baseball cards. Lawn-mowing money and a small allowance would combine to buy as many packs as possible. Topps baseball cards came in packs of 12 and cost 20 cents per pack. Often called "wax packs" after the wax-coated paper the cards were wrapped in, the 1978 set consisted of 726 cards.

My "wax packs" to sort through for waste week were the seven waste receptacles in our home: one in the kitchen, two from the bathrooms, one in the laundry room and one each in the kids' bedrooms.

A couple of dollars would net six or seven baseball packs, a 10-cent popsicle, and some Swedish fish in a small brown paper bag. Snacks in hand, Tom and I would rush out to the front stoop to open the packs. It was like Christmas morning opening each pack hoping the rare cards would somehow show up. All Stars and well-known players like Jim Palmer, Pete Rose, George Brett, Thurman Munson, Tom Seaver, Dave Winfield, Jim Rice, and Rod Carew would cause celebration of found treasure. Others like Wayne Twitchell, John Denny, Mike Vail, Terry Harmon, Larry Demery, and Bill North were met with silence and a quick move to the next pack.

The rigid plastic milk bottles, cardboard boxes, and food scraps were the All Stars—these items fit nicely into the circular economy of materials. Paper plates lathered in peanut butter, oil-soaked pizza boxes, and candy wrappers made of disparate materials were the no-name players I lamented having to sort.

Tom and I would look through the cards like an auto shuffler on the Vegas Strip. A thin, stiff piece of bubble gum also came in each pack. We would jam the pink rectangle into our mouths just before grabbing the next pack. It was a tornado of excitement, wrappers, disappointment, and garbled conversation as the wad of gum grew.

When I got back home, the first stop was to weave new cards in with my existing annual collection in my Topps Sports vinyl storage locker. The case was maroon, about the size of a laptop computer but a bit wider and was wallpapered with action shots from various sports. Twisting a metal clasp released the two shutters that enclosed the contents. Opening the two panels revealed two columns and multiple rows of slots for placing cards. My cards were always arranged by team.

For waste week, my four bins and compost bowl were my organizing mechanism to get all materials that follow the same waste path in the same place.

I would place my new cards with their teammates already in the case. Arranging by team made it easy to identify a duplicate—any duplicates were set aside for trading. I would also log the number of the card. To complete the collection, I needed to get all 726. The whole collection made each card valuable, even the ones I was less excited about upon opening.

Similarly, if we have a goal of a circular economy, there is no waste. We view every piece of waste as a resource and therefore treat it as valuable.

This was an ongoing process that began anew each year with a new set of cards, new players, and a new card locker to fill. While I did not think about the value of the collection at the time, I now know the condition and organization of the cards matters.

A pile of baseball cards that are battered and mixed without regard to team, year, or number are far less valuable than ones that are in pristine condition and are well organized.

Sorting waste like I sorted baseball cards was the goal. Just like every card had value and a place in my Topps collection locker, I tried to look at each piece of waste as valuable and find a defined place for it to go to remain in the circular economy if possible. Sorting baseball cards was entirely reliant on me. What I realized was that sorting waste was not.

I tried to have my family be wary of dumping food scraps or any kind of liquid (nail polish, toothpaste, oils, soda etc.) into the receptacles throughout the house. I had a separate bowl set aside to collect organic waste and asked that liquids be emptied in the sink prior to disposal of the package. I wanted to avoid the mess of sifting through wet, cross-contaminated waste but that mainly fell on ears more in tune with convenience than conservation. I found myself understanding the challenge of waste separation on a mass scale as I picked through recyclable paper and plastics that were likely no longer recyclable because of liquid contamination.

After seven days of separating, weighing, and logging data, these were the results:

- 45% of waste by weight was recycled either through curbside pickup or returning plastic bags to the in-store drop-off

- 20% was waste I could not salvage and was thus bound for landfill

- 32% of waste was food, all of which was turned into compost

- 3% of the waste was captured and reused

Let's look at each of these percentages.

45% of our waste could be recycled. The recycle bin was the most popular end destination. Our recycled waste was more than double our landfill waste. By the week's end, I was physically getting into the recycle bin to compact it—jumping up and down to create more space. Struggling to fit all the recyclables in the bin while seeing plenty of space in the landfill bin was encouraging and was the opposite of a normal week.

When we recycle, we likely do so for two reasons: to feel good and/or to avoid guilt. We feel good that the item going into the bin will be sorted, made into something else, and resold to begin the cycle again. We avoid the guilt that can accompany our society's focus on consumption. We want to play a role in helping items to find a new path. But when recyclables are picked up, what really happens next?

Seeing a news story about items thought of as being recyclable winding up in landfill or worse, in the natural environment, begins to sow seeds of doubt about the whole recycling system. When recyclers cannot find a buyer for collected and sorted recyclables, particularly mixed bales, often their only option is landfill. The system is hard to fully understand. How can something that we think is recyclable not get recycled? It is frustrating when we as households do our part, yet it does not always flow the way we may think or intend.

In the early days of recycling in the United States, the consumer had multiple bins to sort waste into prior to pick up—glass, paper, metal etc. In general, recycling rates with the burden on the consumer to sort was low. To increase participation, single-stream recycling was rolled out. Recycling rates increased as the consumer benefited from only two choices: trash or recycle. However, the simplicity of the choice sacrifices the effectiveness of the recycling—it exacerbates contamination in the aggregated mixed mountain of materials to process. According to the National Waste and Recycling Association, on average, an estimated 25% of the stuff in the recycle steam is too contaminated to go anywhere but the landfill.[37]

Single-stream recycling pushes the sorting burden onto the processing centers to separate the incoming materials. The goal of sorting is to gain the purest possible bale per material type in order to re-sell it. The purer the bale, the more likely it is to sell and work itself back into feedstock for future products.

In the last 20 years, the volume of recyclable materials has increased. Products vary more widely in physical make-up, and increasingly come in a plastic and/or flexible packaging. For example, raisins, which used to be packed in boxes, now come in stand-up pouches. Ketchup used to be packaged in glass bottles and now comes in plastic containers. Eggs came in cardboard crates and now come in rigid plastic packaging.

Here's an example of how and why some packaging has changed: Sour cream was originally packaged in glass jars, then plastic containers, and now can be found in stand-up pouches. The flexible pouch offers four unique properties that rigid containers do not.

1. <u>Longer shelf life once opened</u>. When sour cream is exposed to air, it begins to spoil. The stand-up pouch's unique method of dispensing through an airtight slit eliminates exposure to air of the remaining product in the tube, so the sour cream lasts longer.

2. <u>Reduced product waste.</u> By squeezing only the necessary contents from the tube and keeping the rest of the sour cream fresh, there's a greater chance of using all the product before it spoils and therefore reducing food waste.

3. <u>Less weight</u>. The tube weighs less and takes up less room in production, transport, and manufacturing than alternative packaging. Less weight means lower transport costs and fewer transportation emissions.

4. <u>Reduced emissions in manufacturing</u>. In general, when a package cannot be avoided, flexible packaging often has a smaller carbon footprint in a life cycle analysis than many alternatives.[38]

There are two other main drivers for flexible packaging to have found its way onto store shelves.

In 2002 the *New York Times* published a prophetic article about waste citing two primary factors in future waste generation trends: Cost reduction, which means making items lighter and easier to transport; and convenience, making items easier for the consumer to use. Flexibles are generally less costly and more convenient and have thus proliferated.[39]

Flexible packaging, then, is cheaper, more convenient, and in general has lower emissions in production than many alternatives. The problem with flexible packaging comes at the end of life. The 45% of waste I was able to recycle was primarily a mix of paper, cardboard, some glass, rigid plastic containers, plastic bags, and metal cans. The stand-up pouches and snack bags were forced into the landfill bin. So why can't they be recycled?

20% of our waste was bound for landfill. The landfill-bound waste created during the week came primarily from three categories.

First was contaminated waste due to poor sorting by our household—waste that could have been rescued but was contaminated with liquids or food, which our municipality's current waste infrastructure cannot recycle. Examples were numerous and messy in discovery. Paper soaked with soda, boxes stained with coffee grinds, newspaper with wet eggshell residue, paper towels soaked in grease, plastic bags with chicken bones and guts, plastic trays with meat blood or magazines with pizza sauce splattered on the cover all were forced into the landfill bin.

Second was waste that could not be recycled due to the product having been used for its purpose such as tissues, napkins, paper towels, small candy wrappers, plastic cling wrap, and tin foil.

Contamination with food, grease, and bodily fluids are unable to be "cleaned" during most recycling processes. I was alarmed at the amount of disposable paper products we used. Of the 20% of our landfill waste, 8% was tied to used paper products. We had previously eliminated our household use of disposable plastic water bottles and paper plates. Following our week's experiment, we decided to try to reduce and/or replace napkins, paper towels, and tissues with reusable napkins, towels, and hankies that we can wash.

Third was waste made of disparate materials. For example, paper laminated to plastic in a stand-up pouch or metal combined with plastic in a snack bag. The combined materials are great for freshness, unique aesthetics, and a longer shelf life but are very difficult to separate and to recycle economically. A potato chip bag is a multi-layer structure that provides a barrier to oxygen, grease, and light to keep the chips fresh until the bag is opened. The burst of potato scent that invades the senses and whets the appetite when opening the bag is made possible by the packaging. Even flexible packaging made of similar materials that may in fact be technically recyclable may not be friendly additions to recycling facilities without updated equipment to process the rigid packaging of old.

32% was food waste. I was surprised by the high percentage of food waste—one-third of our waste by weight. Roughly a quarter of the composted waste came from unavoidable sources—banana peels, vegetable trimmings like carrot and celery ends, meat cut-offs like fat prior to cooking, and coffee grinds. About 25% came from food scraps left on plates after meals. The rest was generated from expired food—leftovers that were never consumed, unopened products that went past the date on the package, or food in the pantry that was opened and grew stale. Awareness of how much food we were throwing away made us all think about how we could reduce our food waste—making less to avoid having excess per meal, batch cooking, eating more leftovers, checking the pantry before shopping to avoid duplicate buying, and closing opened bags tightly to help reduce the potential for stale product.

Every night the Lomi machine was busy turning food waste into compost. I would load the machine and sprinkle the resulting compost in the woods around my house the next day.

3% was reused. A small percentage of items wound up in the trash that I intercepted from landfill to repurpose or reroute to a new home: two old white T-shirts were repurposed as cleaning rags, three used books were good enough to be brought to our local thrift store, an old hose was reevaluated. It was over 10 years old and had a few minor leaks, but I could still use it for the limited amount of use it got. While the reuse category was small, it had a big effect on my mindset for the week. I found myself trying not to waste things and reusing them instead so I did not have to count them at night!

Sorting the variety of waste materials generated by my household was not an insignificant task. The experience of trying to mimic what recycling facilities do every day gave me a great appreciation for their work. I visited a couple—County Waste and Recycling in Albany, NY and Napa Recycling and Composting Facility in Napa, CA. I was able to watch as mountains of material from thousands of curbside single-stream recycle bins were fed through conveyor belts and various sorting mechanisms. At the end, the materials were separated into general types. While some bales appeared to be purer, others were more mixed. Mixed bales have limited value. Tour guides at each facility provided color to what we were seeing.

While many items go on to be recycled, there are plenty of discarded items that do not. Some materials the recycling center receives are not recyclable, some are not easily recycled, some are contaminated with organics, and the infrastructure to support this waste management is not yet fully developed. These are the type of items that wind up in landfills and are thus a source of frustration when highlighted in the news. The mix of mitigating factors creates confusion, mistrust, and holes in the recycling system.

UNDERSTANDING RECYCLING

Recyclability needs to meet three criteria. It must be collected efficiently, processed in a recycling facility, and have viable end markets to be sold in. Fixing the recycling system is a mixed bag of ideas that, although ostensibly simple, are hard to implement due to multiple stakeholders, the wide variety of waste, and funding required. The experience of cataloging my household waste for a week helped me to identify some ways to help reduce waste or make waste more circular and in effect help recycling centers create more usable products.

1. Design with the end in mind. Designing products with the result of a no-waste end-of-life will eliminate non-recyclable by-products from falling out of the circular economy. Designing products and packaging with the target of reducing, reusing, composting, or recycling increases circularity and reduces waste to landfill.

2. Invest in recycling infrastructure. Packaging advances have outpaced advances in recycling processing. Glass bottles, aluminum cans, and hard plastic bottles are more easily and widely recycled than flexible stand-up pouches, small wrappers, and plastic bags. Advances in equipment to handle a wider array of materials will increase circularity. The challenge is finding the dollars for investment.

To date, producers of materials have mostly stayed on the sidelines of material recovery, privatizing profits and socializing costs. Responsibility for recycling cannot solely rest with the consumer to do their part and neither can recycling processors be left to invest on their own. Government legislation to enforce recycled content percentages and aid consumers' ability to compost, along with producers funding investment in infrastructure to process the materials they make, are essential to achieving a circular system. The entire supply chain and consumption stream both must play a role if we're to close more loops to circularity.

3. Change the language. Instead of referring to a product as recyclable or not recyclable, change the language to how circular the item is or can be. By changing the language, we can start to change the mindset. When we say recycle, we really mean we want the product to be circular in nature and stay in the economy. A highly recyclable or compostable item is not necessarily circular. A highly circular product, on the other hand, is easily and readily composted or recycled either to make the same thing or something else.

Here's an example: A small candy wrapper is most likely recyclable, but the package is so small, there is little value in its collection. Most wrappers are therefore land-filled, so a candy wrapper is not likely circular.

Communicating the circularity of a product or package on the package would further educate the consumer, place additional demand on manufacturers to make more circular products, and ultimately do what the word "recycle" was meant to do from the start.

Recycling and composting are the digestive system of a consumption society. A strong recycling and composting system provide a path to reducing waste (by using it to make or grow other things), reduces environmental pressures (greenhouse gas emissions), and contributes to the larger availability of resources (by reusing existing materials). The goal is to use existing or renewable materials at creation with a defined end-of-life to keep the material in the circular economy.

Circularity is likely what we really mean when we say and participate in recycling and composting. Maybe it is the word we should start using.

4. Request recycled content in products. If we are not buying recycled content, we are not recycling. In other words, if we buy based on the item containing recycled content, the manufacturer will be forced to buy the recycled material from processors who in turn will seek out sources for recyclables. The demand will drive supply and investments throughout the supply chain.

5. Narrow the price gap between virgin and recycled content resins. Virgin resin to make plastics from fossil fuels is generally cheaper than post-consumer recycled content resins.[40] It will be hard for recycled resins to take a stronghold in the market until the cost differential is reduced, eliminated, or offset. Policy mandating a certain percentage of recycled content and/or taxing fossil fuel-based materials can each help reduce the price gap.

6. Improve product labeling. The recycling information on the labels we looked at during waste week varied widely: from no labeling at all regarding the end-of-life path for the package to the generic chasing arrows to highly detailed "How2recycle" labeling. The standardization of labeling would likely go a long way to recyclable packages avoiding landfill.

Nutrition labels may offer a guide. Nutrition information was not always required on food packaging and beverages prior to 1990. The United States Nutrition Facts first label appeared in 1994. The labels are now a reliable source of information to help consumers make more informed choices through standardized disclosures of ingredients.[41] The labels all look the same regardless of the package. My hope is that end-of-life labeling can follow a similar path to standardization.

6. Eliminate the package. If a product's packaging is not needed for branding, protection, nutritional information, safety instructions, or directions of use, don't package the item. Lush is a beauty care products company focused on reducing packaging. About 65% of their year-round products are unpackaged, or as they say, "naked." In 2005 Lush shampoo bars switched from being packaged in plastic bottles to naked. Since then, they have sold 41 million shampoo bars saving 3,417 tons of plastic from ever being produced.[42]

7. Change the business model. Reusable and refillable products significantly reduce the need for packaging. Spruce is a UK cleaning products company whose mission is to help people live free from harsh chemicals and toxic plastics. The products are sold in reusable aluminum bottles with small refillable cleaning concentrate packs. Water is mixed with the concentrate in the reusable bottle to form the cleaning solution. If every UK household switched to refillable cleaning products, 300 million single plastics bottles could be eliminated.[43]

8. Compost. Composting waste is the unknown star without a stage to perform on. Organic waste (food scraps, garden waste, grass trimmings, etc.) in anaerobic landfills generates CO_2 and methane, a potent greenhouse gas. The EPA states that "by composting wasted food and other organics, methane emissions are significantly reduced."[44]

One-third of all food produced worldwide each year is wasted or lost. If food waste was represented as its own country, it would be the third largest greenhouse gas emitter behind the United States and China.[45]

Why composting is important seems obvious. How to do it is more of a challenge. While a composting mindset and infrastructure to support organic waste streams does exist in some places, in most places it does not. Without education as to what can and cannot be composted, without home compost facilities, without appliances like Lomi being affordable and available, and without a viable curbside pickup, composting will remain a fringe performer on the circular stage.

9. Chemical Recycling. Mechanical recycling is the process that drives the recycling industry today. Mechanical processes like separating, washing, drying, grinding, re-granulating, and compounding turn waste into feedstock for new items to be made. Chemical recycling refers to any re-processing technology that turns waste into its original monomer. The monomer can then be used to make other items. In returning the waste to its original form, the new product formed is "like-new." Chemical recycling can be used on hard to recycle items like mixed materials. When waste is put through the eight previous strainers and still needs a place to go, chemical recycling offers an option. Today, chemical recycling takes many forms, is expensive, and is not yet at scale. It is only a complement to the others above, not a substitute.

So, let's compare what I experienced from my household waste experiment with the national statistics.

Americans produce 4.9 lbs of waste per person per day. We each produced just 1.8 lbs. At the national average our family of five would have produced 171.5 lbs, whereas we totaled only 63.1 lbs. My urge to pat us all on the back was muted knowing my teenage sons were rarely home that week, our youngest was at camp for four of the days, we did not bring home our waste to count when we left the house for work or recreation, and I spent a lot of my time counting waste, not creating it.

The following week we cleaned out our basement, which resulted in overflowing bins. My guess is it offset the low week we experienced and suddenly 4.9 lbs per person per day does not seem too outlandish. Regardless, the American number is far higher than places like Brazil (2.3 lbs) and India (0.75 lbs).[46] There is no ignoring perhaps the biggest hurdle encountered thus far—many developed countries' ravenous consumption, which results in ballooning emissions and mountains of waste.

32% of waste is recycled or composted. In our waste week we recycled or composted 77% of the waste we created. Our rate crushed the national average.

A Ball Foundation study, "The 50 States of Recycling," looked at recycling rates for common containers and packaging materials (CCPM) by state, with and without cardboard. The cardboard is teased out as it is the most commonly recycled material. New York is 51% without and 58% with cardboard. Maine is the highest at 72% without and 74% with. Thirty states are below 33% recycling rates without cardboard with a few states less than 5%.[47]

Teasing out rates by state helps avoid some misguided common narratives about recycling rates. Low aggregated recycling rates sap enthusiasm and push people to give up on the whole idea even if in certain areas it is working better.

75% of Americans' waste stream is recyclable. Taking out composted waste, we were able to recycle 68% of the remaining waste. If not for the cross contamination, that percentage would be higher—75% seems reasonable.

The 4.9 lbs of waste generated per person per day and 32% materials recycled statistics speak to the power of convenience. It requires less effort to throw away a paper plate than to wash a reusable one. It is easier to stuff used garments in the landfill bin for weekly collection than to find someone or someplace who could use the donation. It is quicker to throw a plastic bread bag into the trash than to clean it out and bring it back to the in-store drop-off at a local store. I experienced all these scenarios. Throwing things away without much thought versus meticulously sorting at the source for maximum recovery was a difference of a few hours over the course of a week.

The 75% statistic speaks to design. If not compostable, making all waste entirely recyclable at least gives it a chance to be recycled. Due to the mix of materials in products and packaging, however, 25% of waste remains unrecyclable. Today, reaching a 75% recycle rate would appear to be short of the goal but in actuality it would be the maximum rate attainable in a typical mechanical recycling facility.

We did not manage to achieve a perfectly circular system where waste from one process turns into a feedstock for the next but we got closer than I had previously thought we would. We diverted 80% of our waste away from landfill. Our family's reduced waste to landfill made us feel good but we also knew our efforts depended on what happens next. We are just one small link in the chain. With no control over what happens after we do our part, the actual path of resources depends on the rest of the system.

Our efforts to divert waste away from landfill felt like building a castle on an ocean beach at low tide. As time passes and the tide comes in, the sandcastle and our motivation to rebuild it is washed away. Without the same energy to build again, the intuition to build further back up the beach, the education to understand tide patterns, or the idea of using a different building material, the efforts will never accumulate into building something that lasts.

At the very least, I was able to answer the question, "What can I do to help?"

At most, maybe it provides a path for others to look at their own situation and answer the same question the best they can. If we all can answer the question and be consistent in our answer, we can build momentum toward positive change.

In 2021 Sustainabilitymag.com posted an article, "Ten countries tackling plastic pollution." Germany was ranked first in waste management and recycling. It recycles 70% of all waste produced—the highest rate in the world. A mix of smart and consistent waste policies, producer responsibility for packaging put into the market, and a defined five-bin system for consumers at disposal combine to create an efficient flow of materials.[48] Germany has shown if systems are in place to support sorting, it can be done.

My experiment revealed a reason to get into the boat—personal actions can make a difference. Personal actions like sorting waste, reducing consumption when possible, and being more thoughtful at disposal. In taking time to put things in their proper place, my mind blocked the idea of waste being "disposable."

Personal actions, connectivity, community, understanding path dependence, the circular economy framework, and guilt. I'd identified six reasons to get into your boat.

However, the experience also uncovered three more obstacles to overcome—consumption, convenience, and cost. These three heavyweights joined a growing list of bandits: selfishness, ownership, not in my backyard, small actions as irrelevant, and ignorance. Eight thieves stealing attention from the unaware.

As I uncovered reasons not to get into the boat, reasons I tried to refute regularly, I realized I was unaware that I was among the unaware. My journey was turning into a search I had not anticipated. The thieves were beginning to tip the scales toward inaction. More suspects were being identified to undermine the reasons to find sustainability. Rounding them up for questioning was as important as finding more reasons. Up until that point, Nassau Lake had been my primary source to uncovering both.

That was about to change.

Chapter 7

SILENT SUMMER

knew my experience at Nassau Lake was not isolated. Many locations across the country had their own environmental degradation issues. Each with a gut-wrenching, mostly unresolved story. My attention shifted to traveling to some of these places. But before visiting other affected areas, I first wanted to visit a place that was seemingly unencumbered by pollution to reveal an ideal state of nature.

I arrived at the Rachel Carson Wildlife Refuge on the southern coast of Maine just after the visitor center closed. The trails remained open to visitors until sunset. I walked the wide, winding, packed dirt trail alone on the second day of summer. Kids still in their last week of school combined with the 5:30 p.m. start time emptied the refuge of other visitors. There was no competition for views at lookout points, no need to socially distance, and no invisible urge to move along that a crowd invariably creates.

Sunlight from the west fought through the canopy of eastern white pines and hemlocks, which outnumbered the oaks and maples. Ferns dominated the groundcover. The trail meanders through a deciduous forest bordering an open expanse extending to the ocean. The winding rivers in the expanse are the first link between fresh water from the woodlands mixing with seawater from ocean tides. This transition zone is also where the vegetation changes from trees to salt meadow cordgrass. This meeting of habitats forms spectacular views of a variety of natural environments—tidal marshes, coastal meadows, beach and dune, rocky coast, and forest.

Wooden-planked structures extend out from the forest in 10 places along the trail. The structures felt like docks in a lake where standing at the end offered more panoramic views than could be had without. While moored boats typically accompany docks to allow for full immersion into the scene, the Carson Trail structures did not. The end of the lookouts were as close as you could get to the protected landscape. The limitation was satisfying. Being there was a privilege.

The refuge was established in 1966 to protect valuable salt marshes and estuaries for migratory birds. A huge variety of plants and wildlife filled the 14,000 acres. This was their home, and I was a visitor. My inclusion any further than the edge of the dock would be unwelcome.

Rachel Carson, the refuge's namesake, wrote *Silent Spring* in 1962, a book that changed the course of how lawmakers and the public viewed chemicals. The title says it all. Toxic chemicals—specifically DDT (dichloro-diphenyl-trichloroethane)—used in the 1950s and 1960s to control insects were affecting far more than just the pests. The result of their use was cancer, wildlife fatalities, and overall environmental degradation. The sounds of spring were silenced by the chemicals.

I walked the same trail the following morning. While the sounds of strong ocean winds blowing leaves and tall pines had dominated the refuge the night prior, the sounds of wildlife took center stage on my morning walk.

Life was everywhere. A snowy egret stood erect in the smooth cordgrass growing along the distant riverbank. Upon folding its legs and angling its isosceles-shaped head down to fish, I could no longer identify the white dot as a bird without my binoculars. Chipmunks darted across the marked trail before slowing once out of the danger zone. Fifteen geese sat at the crux of two tidal rivers in the shorter salt meadow grass as if enjoying a morning coffee while making plans for the day to come. A hawk glided toward me far above before my line of sight was blocked by the height of the trees to my rear.

Sounds abounded. Some high, some low. Some consistent, some not. All combined to define a wide variety of animals my untrained ear could not identify. I did not speak their language, but I was an enthusiastic listener.

Eastern sandpipers, tree swallows, loons, great blue herons, piping plovers, Canadian geese, American black ducks, herring gulls, rock pigeons, red-tailed hawks, downy woodpeckers, kestrel falcons, bald eagles, and northern saw-whet owls were amongst the 250-plus birds listed in the visitor center's information pamphlets.

The diversity and varied frequency of that many bird calls offers an endless combination of sound. This concert setlist changes all through the day and night. It is never the same. Different birds join and bow out depending on the time of day, month, and season.

Carson's book set a new path for regulation surrounding pesticides and chemicals in the environment. Rachel Carson saw things we did not see at the time. The chemicals being used as pesticides were killing the pests but were also having far reaching effects on the rest of the environment.

Her work sparked the creation of the Environmental Protection Agency's fast-tracked legislation toward clean water and clean air and raised awareness to the extent her work is often viewed as the 20th century's most influential environmental book. Thanks to her campaigning, many of the birds most affected by DDT made extraordinary comebacks.[49]

I returned again and again to Nassau Lake to paddle, to bike, and to think. If Rachel Carson had written about it, the book would likely have been called *Silent Summer*. The silence on the lake was deafening. The surface calm of the water belied the poison below.

Over the years 46,000 tons of waste were dumped at the landfill. Solvents, waste oils, polychlorinated biphenyls (PCB), sludges, and solids. PCBs are a group of synthetic organic chemicals made up of hydrogen, carbon, and chlorine atoms. The number and arrangement of the chlorine atoms determines the properties. They were made in the United States from 1929 until their ban in 1979. Due to their chemical stability, non-flammability, high boiling point, and electrical insulation properties, PCBs were used in the manufacture of a wide range of industrial products—pigments, dyes, paints, electrical and heat transfer equipment, adhesives and tapes, cable insulation, caulking, and floor finish.[50] PCBs do not break down readily in the natural environment and can remain in water, soil, and in the air for lengthy periods of time.[51] What's more, PCBs have shown evidence of leading to adverse health effects from metabolic diseases to cancer.[52]

The chemicals in the bottom of the lake got there prior to

the formation of the Environmental Protection Agency (EPA). The new agency consolidated research, standard-setting, monitoring, and policing to protect the environment and was founded to combat a nation at slumber when it came to worrying about pollutants. Its formation was a reaction to a series of environmental disasters, for example Rachel Carson's book about pesticides, an off-shore oil rig spill in California, and chemicals choking the Cuyahoga River in Ohio, all of which spoke to pollutants across the land going unchecked. Another major contributing event was Apollo 8's mission to the Moon in 1968. The first photographs of Earth by a human from space gave people a real sense that Earth was not infinite in its bounty. Limited resources plus multiple examples of generational changing man-made environmental catastrophes contributed to federal government formation of the EPA on December 2, 1970.[53]

Ten years later, in 1980, the federal Superfund program was created in the United States to allocate resources to investigate and clean up contaminated sites nationwide. Superfund sites are listed on the National Priority List (NPL) and can be any kind of site where the government deems the waste hazardous or problematic.

A Substance Priority List (SPL) is revised and published every two years to report substances in order of priority, most commonly found at National Priority List (NPL) Superfund sites. The list tracks chemicals that pose the most significant threat to human and environmental health. The 2022 ranking of the top seven in order are arsenic, lead, mercury, vinyl chloride, polyvinyl chlorinated biphenyls (PCBs), benzene, and cadmium. Toxicity, frequency, and potential for human exposure are the primary factors in determining the highest risk chemicals.[54]

There are currently over 1,300 NPL Superfund sites in the United States. Twenty-one million people (6% of the U.S.

population) live within 1 mile of a Superfund site, and 73,000,000 live within 3 miles (22%).[55]

Every state except North Dakota has at least one active Superfund site. Waste and industry tend to follow people, so if follows that the most populated states have more sites. New Jersey has the most (113 sites) followed by California (97) and Pennsylvania (95).[56]

While there are places on the list that are known by name, many are not. Headland, Alabama; Rancho Cordova, California; New Castle, Delaware; Hialeah, Florida; Lemhi County, Idah; Olathe, Kansas; Corinna, Maine; Ionia, Michigan; Flowood, Mississippi; Yerington, Nevada; Waynesville, North Carolina; The Dalles, Oregon; Whitewood, South Dakota; Perryton, Texas; Marysville, Washington; Evansville, Wyoming; and Nassau, New York are far more prevalent on the list.

From what I had learned, smaller and often more unknown towns seemed to attract the ticking time bombs. In them, waste was looking for a place to hide.

Prospective sites are rated. The Hazardous Ranking System is a scoring system used to assess the relative risk associated with actual or potential releases of hazardous substances from a site based on the information that can be collected. A high score on the Hazardous Ranking System—over 28.5— qualifies that site for listing on the National Priority List.[57] If the ranking is not high enough, it remains a site to clean up but does not qualify for the NPL. In these circumstances, there are other federal and state clean-up programs that can assist.

The time frame for clean-up varies widely. Public pressure, political will, testing/sampling to determine the amount and dif-ficulty of clean-up required, and funding are the major variables that differ from site to site. In the 1980s, over 1,000 sites were added to the National Priority List. About 30 years later, 700 of those original sites remain on the list.[58]

Besides Nassau, my attention was drawn to two other Superfund sites. Love Canal in Niagara Falls, NY and Ottawa County, Oklahoma. I visited both to see if their look, feel, and backstory had similarities to the Nassau story.

Love Canal (named after the developer William T. Love) is a neighborhood within the Niagara Falls, NY city limits. In the late 1800s and early 1900s, a canal was dug to connect the upper and lower Niagara River—approximately 7 miles long. After digging part of the canal, the project was scrapped. The 60-foot wide by 3,000-foot-long trench turned into a municipal and chemical disposal site. Hooker Chemical was among those that used the site for disposal. By the 1950s, the canal was covered with dirt and development began on the site. An elementary school and 800 private single-family homes and 240 apartments were built on and around the former canal.[59] The buried chemicals may have been visibly contained but their ill effects were not.

When people began to complain of being sick, Love Canal turned into a national story. In 1978, then President Jimmy Carter stated the site presented a federal health emergency. Twenty-two thousand tons of buried toxic chemicals were becoming visible in the health of residents and dead plant life surrounding the canal. The 70-acre site registered a 52.23 score on the Hazardous Ranking System. The site went on the National Priority List in 1983.

Two hundred different chemicals were found. Chief among them was benzene. Benzene is a colorless or light-colored liquid at room temperature. It is highly flammable. Benzene is formed through natural processes—mainly volcanoes and forest fires—and is also a natural part of crude oil, gasoline, and cigarette smoke. Some industries used benzene mixed with other chemicals to make resins, nylon, and other synthetic fibers. Benzene was also used to make lubricants, rubbers, dyes, detergents, drugs, and pesticides. "The Department of Health and Human Services (DHHS) has determined that benzene causes cancer in humans. Long-term exposure to high levels of benzene in the air can cause leukemia, cancer of the blood-forming organs."[60]

I visited Love Canal in the summer of 2022. Frontier Avenue, 93rd Street, Colvin Boulevard, and 101st Street form the drivable perimeter of the site. The enclosed rectangular space covers about 15 football fields. As I drove around with the site always to my right, signs of a busy community mixed with ghosts of the past.

To my left on Frontier Avenue was a major highway where cars zipped along likely without a thought of chemicals or dated health issues. From 93rd Street, a glance out the driver's side window saw residential homes, and tree-lined side streets forming suburban neighborhoods. Colvin Boulevard offered the busiest streets, small convenient stores, traffic and pedestrians, revealing signs of busy life. The final street of enclosure was 101st Street, which ran parallel to 93rd Street, eight blocks to the east.

101st street was unkept—a large number of potholes formed a natural speed reduction system, weeds sprouting in every available crack made the pavement uneven, and the road had narrowed with the passage of time as nature invaded from the sides. Abandoned lots and a few dilapidated structures filled my view. With the elementary school that once sat just two blocks away on 99th Street on my mind, I tried to picture how busy this place was during the 1950s and 1960s. The neighborhood I saw surrounding 93rd Street was clearly once replicated here on 101st. Having driven around the perimeter, it was time to get closer.

There is an 8-foot chain high-link fence that forms a tighter perimeter around the site. Cement barriers on 100th Street prohibited cars so I got out and approached on foot for a better view.

My brain saw a prison—the space contained, guarded for community protection—so I put my nose through the fence, which gave me an unfettered view. An open field of grass and bright sunlight in a brilliant blue sky captured the stage. A few mature trees framed the view. Birds swooping and summer cicadas singing completed the picture. I imagined what it would have looked like in times past—a busy schoolyard, children playing, laughter. As I stepped back to the prison view, the reality of what was and what is butted up against one another.

I had driven all around the site, walked as close as I could to the site, but I could not go inside to experience the site for myself. A mentor from my past turned out to be my window to what lay on the other side of the fence.

Linda Krzykowski is a lifelong educator serving in many roles at the University at Albany for 30 years. She is the best kind of educator. One completely interested in the student. One that leaves the door open to her students for a lifetime. She was my professor 20 years ago and has remained a mentor and now a friend as we have stayed connected through the years. I knew she was from the Buffalo area, so I mentioned my interest in Love Canal. Linda grew up a few blocks from Love Canal. I had hit the jackpot. Time to take her to lunch to get inside the fence.

"When were you aware of the issue at Love Canal?" I asked.

"I was unaware of any real problem until the summer of 1978 when I returned home from college," Linda replied.

"Did you go to the elementary school on the site?"

"Yes. I walked to 93rd Street elementary school from our house on Pasadena Avenue. The school actually had a pool in the basement."

"A pool?" I asked, surprised.

"Yup. How great is that? I took swimming lessons from a young age in the pool," she added.

We went on to talk about how the school pool was likely sitting on or could potentially have even penetrated the clay cap originally put on top of the chemicals when they were buried.

"Who do you hold responsible for what happened?" I asked.

"My grandfather worked for Hooker Chemical. He relayed that Hooker did nothing illegal at the time. 'At the time' seems the key."

We agreed that one's immediate reaction is to hold Hooker Chemical responsible but the closer you look, the more and more you see how much responsibility there is to spread around.

"How did the chemicals affect you and your family living so close to the site?" I asked.

"My family wanted to sell their house but could not. Who was going to buy a house near Love Canal in the late 70s and 80s? The house finally sold but it took over a decade."

Linda told me neither she nor her family experienced any health concerns they know of as a direct result of the chemicals, but she said that some people she knew can likely trace some health problems back to the chemicals.

As we ended our lunch date, I showed her a Google map on my phone of the present-day site. Her eyes lit up as I handed my phone to her. She began to scan the area intently, zooming in and out and scrolling the map to find some landmarks to get her bearings. She narrated what we were looking at, pointing out where the school sat, where her uncle lived, where the ball field was, and ultimately where her house was. She zoomed in on her house and then we "walked" the streets from her house to the place her school used to sit. As she scrolled, I remained silent. She was taking a trip down memory lane, and I was a grateful passenger. This was her home.

My trip to Love Canal ended with one final sweep of the area, driving along roads further from the site. On 102nd Street, just three blocks from the fenced in area, very few homes still stood. One forced me to stop. The small home appeared to be inhabited. I wondered about all they must have gone through to stay—the health concerns, home value, and mental anguish all form up into a monster that never truly leaves you alone. I sat in my car and felt deep admiration for whoever was inside. A sign hung on the front porch just above the walkway to the front door.

"Home Sweet Home."

I welled up inside as I drove away.

Ottawa County is in northeastern Oklahoma. The town of Picher sits inside Ottawa County. Lead and zinc mining dominated the area from 1900 to 1960 when the metals were used by the United States for making bullets during both World Wars. According to local news sources, nearly half the lead and zinc used during World War I was produced in the area.[61]

The mining companies left behind open chat piles. Chat is waste rejected in the lead–zinc milling process. The piles were heavily contaminated by metals, cadmium, and others. For every 1 ton of ore extracted, approximately 16 tons of chat and tailings were left behind.[62] Over the years, mining and milling produced more than 500 million tons of waste in the area.[63] The elevated levels of these metals in the air leached into the soil and found their way into ponds, streams, and lakes. The underground mines also filled with water, which rose to the surface, also contaminated.

In large quantities these heavy metals, particularly lead, cadmium, and zinc, are harmful and toxic to people and wildlife. Prolonged exposure to them led to serious health problems such as unsafe levels of lead in the blood, and higher rates of chronic lung disease for residents in the 40 square mile area.[64] Eventually, in 1983, Picher was put on the National Priority List with a Hazardous Ranking System score of 58.15.

The town of Picher today is a "ghost" town. In 2009, the EPA deemed it unlivable—there was just too much to fix and too high a health risk to stay. The Quapaw Native Americans, who originally owned the land, leased it to mining companies in the first half of the 20th century. Over a century later, all that's left behind is a Superfund site. In 2013, the tribe entered an agreement with the EPA to self-perform the remediation of historic and culturally significant tribal property. The tribe has excavated, hauled, and disposed of over 1.5 million tons of chat as of a few years ago. This is the first ever tribal-led Superfund clean-up in the nation.[65] The original caretakers of the land were now taking ownership of the generational mess.

I visited Picher in June of 2022. Dozens of giant chat piles scattered throughout the town form the skyline. The piles of white chalky grit are a fat conical shape—like the sand that accumulates at the bottom of an hourglass. Some as tall as 150 feet and as wide as a few hundred yards. With one hill rolling into the next, the piles transported my mind to the National Seashore running up the eastern shoreline of Cape Cod. The heaping piles engulfed the town where remaining buildings were either spray painted "Keep Out," had trees growing through the roof, or vines slowly digesting the unkept structure. With no windows, nature had easy access and moved right on in.

The side streets of Picher were narrowed as vegetation butted up against and spilled onto the once two-lane village streets. There were few street signs, no road markings, and no streetlights. There was no need—there was no traffic to control. Houses were few and far between. The once crowded neighborhood had lost most of its buildings either by government relocation of the houses themselves, or a 2008 tornado that served as the final straw for people to move.

People should have a choice whether to leave their hometown under their own volition or never leave at all. The people of Picher did not have that choice. They were asked to evacuate their homes with government relocation and buy-outs.

My interest in Picher led me to University of Oklahoma environmental scientist Robert Nairn. His work for the past 20-plus years has focused on restoring the health of the waterways around Picher. I connected with Robert on the phone to find out more about clean-up sites like Picher, like Nassau Lake.

"How did you become interested in Picher, Oklahoma?" I asked.

"In the late 1990s, the EPA deemed the waters to be irreversible damaged—too big to fix and too costly to fix," Robert stated.

"The word 'irreversible' stuck with me. That did not seem right," he added.

"What have you been doing to make the 'irreversible' reversible?" I asked.

"We have designed and installed two passive water treatment systems in Tar Creek. [Tar Creek is the waterway that runs through the affected towns.] We created various ponds and wetlands to naturally clean the water—it's more complex than this but essentially, we use our understanding of ecology to create human-made ecosystems to clean the water. It's all powered by sun, wind, and principles of biogeochemistry," he said.

"Can this idea be scaled?" I asked, thinking about cleaning the waters of Nassau Lake.

"Yes. Our current system is 3 to 6 acres. We have one in the works that is 120 acres."

Robert and his team's efforts to naturally clean the water gave me hope. Hope that Superfund sites had advocates working on natural solutions.

"Why did the EPA go to this extreme? To evacuate?" I asked.

"As you are probably aware with regard to Nassau, the issue is more than just technical, it is social, cultural, economic, and political—a very complex mix of issues. It took decades to create the problems at Tar Creek, and it will take decades to solve them. The challenges are vast and can seem overwhelming in scale, time, and money. However, I believe nothing is irreversible if we all work together. One of the most concerning issues is that we have not done so," Robert said.

This last comment from an expert was disturbing to me. Cynically, I took the comment to mean many regulators believed if we did nothing, the problem would go away in time. Perhaps a long time.

Before I left to head two and a half hours north to Kansas City Airport, I drove the side streets of Picher that turned off the main road. Even though my eyes saw an abandoned town, my brain saw a skinny paperboy struggling to stay upright, two friends opening baseball card packs on the stoop in front of a mini grocery store, and a local pizza shop. These streets were once alive and are connected to the streets of a similar sized town 1,347 miles away to the northeast—Nassau, NY.

My final stop in Oklahoma took in a remnant of the past. Off the side of the main road sits an 8-foot statue of a gorilla. The Picher High School Gorillas were the 1A football state champions in 1984. The statue of the gorilla recognizing the championship somehow survived the evacuated town and schools and made its way to the primary road that runs through town. Statues symbolize what people from the past choose to remember, memorialize and/or celebrate. Something to be proud of, something that involves a lot of people, something that represents a community. Picher, OK was the home to so many generations of people. In some ways, that legacy of community is still there.

Rachel Carson's Wildlife Preserve is clean, accessible, and thriving within the boundaries of the protected land.

Love Canal, Picher, Oklahoma, and Nassau Lake are polluted, off-limits, and struggling to undo what was done within its boundaries.

My experiences learning about and visiting Love Canal, Picher, and Nassau evoked a common sadness at each place. I saw both what was and what is no longer. A high school football game in Picher, a schoolyard in Love Canal, and a girl skiing on Nassau Lake are now all just memories.

Also, the more I spoke to people, the more I was also gaining a sense of a much more disturbing feeling.

Chapter 8

NUMB

The chemical dumping site on the outskirts of Nassau spans approximately 19 acres. Its Hazardous Ranking System score was 50 and the site was added to the National Priority List in 2011.

The path-dependent event for Nassau Lake began when my grandparents were 36, and my parents were eight. Seventy years later, my young kids still must stay out of the lake. The effects of pollution are measured in generations not years and alarmingly, the expectation for clean-up is "less toxic" not "completely clean." The scar cannot disappear for Nassau nor other Superfund sites. The effects over a long period of time have a numbing effect on people.

"Contaminated Sites Shorten Life Expectancies, Increasing Need for Superfund Clean-ups," was a Forbes, May 2021 headline. A University of Houston study documented what people had long suspected: life expectancy is reduced if a Superfund site is in your neighborhood.[66] Headlines like this feel urgent but when nothing is done or progress snails along, it becomes easy to grow indifferent.

Could 1,300-plus Superfund sites all have been created because of bad actors, ignorance, or just the path of least resistance? Were the people using and promoting the use of DDT in Rachel Carson's book all bad, unknowing, or just going with the flow? Many Superfund sites are the results of common hazardous waste disposal practices in the 1800s through the 1960s.

Manufacturing waste was buried underground, piped to waterways, or just left behind. A 2016 EPA blog post states:

"This was not unlawful at the time, and was probably perceived by most people as perfectly acceptable. They did not realize that, decades later, the soil where they live or the groundwater they rely on as a source of drinking water would be contaminated and unsafe to use."[67]

Too many people made the same dumping decisions. Both private and public entities, in various production markets and in various places, all took part in this means of disposal.[68]

Prior to 1970 with no EPA, there were no chaperones at the dance of disposal. No referees in the game of business. A kaleidoscope of business as usual, ignorance, or choosing to ignore, operating within the law and with no oversight reveals a changing and complex image of accountability, awareness, and decision-making per site. The image we see through the viewing tube to the object box at the end is altered with the slightest change in variables, timing, and perspective.

Take–Make–Dispose—the linear economy has dominated for over a century. Prior to 1970, products were made with little attention to disposal. The disregard led directly to viewing land

and waterways as "single use." By comparison, oversight and laws today make the possibility that what was common in the past is much more unlikely today. Bad players may find loopholes, but they have a harder time using ignorance as a shield. Even players with the best of intentions may still fall victim to the path of least resistance.

The path of least resistance is a common crutch that never goes out of style and is yet another suspect to vet. It carves its way through established regulation, social norms, and popular opinion to establish a clear, natural path. The path is so easy to travel its origins become forgotten. The path acts as a magnet to attract members and once on the path its travelers wear blinders. Other paths are not recognized, not seen, or are labeled as outliers. The outliers know their path well, as they deliberately choose it. The people on the path of least resistance do not know and did not choose.

My trips to Nassau Lake gave me time to think. As I sat alone in my kayak, I looked to the sky for answers and thought of another question. If there is waste below me at the bottom of the lake where we could not see, is there also waste above us I could not see? Back at home, I googled "space garbage" and was amazed at what I found.

There are approximately 100 million pieces of debris about .04 inches (or one millimeter) and larger orbiting the Earth. Around 23,000 pieces are larger than a softball and a half million are about the size of a marble. "Space junk" is the term for any debris left by humans in space. It can be anything from satellites no longer in use or paint chips from rockets. Traveling at speeds of up to 17,500 miles per hour, even tiny paint flecks can cause damage to spacecraft.[69]

Much like the circular thinking for waste that has only just begun on Earth, the same we hope can be applied to space. Policing with only guidelines and goodwill without the support of regulation and laws cannot prevent terrestrial waste from escaping into the Earth's waterways, lands and atmosphere and cannot prevent extra-terrestrial debris from escaping containment in space. Everything goes somewhere.

WHY DO PEOPLE GO NUMB?

Hope of cleaning up Superfund sites, much less preventing future ones, becomes a seemingly Herculean task when you consider that funding for the clean-up programs has declined over the last 20 years.[70]

Environment America reports that from 1999 to 2020, annual funding decreased more than a billion dollars (in constant 2020 dollars) and 34 construction projects did not begin in 2020 because of a lack of appropriations for the Superfund program."[71]

Many current Superfund sites were created prior to recognizing consequences. Evaporating funds, a full understanding of what needs to be cleaned up, and determining accountability for payment all are agents to decelerate progress and elongate the already generational timeline for clean-up.

For the Dewey Loeffel Landfill Superfund site in Nassau, a Community Advisory Group or CAG has been in place for many years. A CAG is a diverse group of community members whose purpose is to provide a forum to present their needs and concerns related to the Superfund decision-making process. I joined the Nassau CAG group calls in 2021.

I began to be exposed to the complexities of cleaning up the site. Of primary concern was the location of waste. The dump site was 2 to 3 miles from the lake. The visible and invisible waterways that led down to the lake swell with precipitation and snow melt. The chemicals move when the water moves and this movement makes a holistic plan to present, fund, and clean up the site a never-ending game of hide and seek. The conversation made me think that the chemicals in the landfill may not be fully contained. I added "containment" to the list of things to find out more about.

With approximately 20 participants on the call, the number of people invested in the process was encouraging. So much information to absorb and understand. I was the rookie on the call. Listening to others helped me begin to better understand the path forward.

Barbara Reina is a Nassau resident who regularly attends CAG meetings. As an independent journalist, she has written articles on the landfill situation and local environmental issues for international publications including *Earth Island Journal*, and regional publications: *The River/Hudson Valley Newsroom* and *Times Union – Hudson Valley*. She is the documentary filmmaker for *Love Canal X 2 | A Landfill Dilemma in Nassau, NY*.

After the call I caught up with Barbara and we talked one-on-one about the chemical containment issue.

"Why do we need water filtration in a landfill?" she asked.

I had never thought about it and responded, "Not sure."

"Residents are still concerned about the condition of the bedrock underneath the former dump site. In the 1980s, state officials installed a cap over it and slurry wall around it without a landfill liner underneath. Natural bedrock, with cracks and fractures, can be pathways to slow leakage of contaminants," Barbara said.

"So, the water filtration is there to try to capture chemicals that leak into waterways?"

"The on-site water treatment facility treats contaminated water from the landfill, then discharges it into the nearby Valatie Kill, sending the treated water downstream," she explained.

Barbara's expertise shone through in our conversation. As we continued talking, the conversation eventually moved on to the human impact of pollution.

"What is the effect on people given the generational time it is taking to fully address the issue?"

"When people don't get what they've been asking for and years go by, they can grow jaded and numb," she said.

"What do they want?"

"They want the contamination from the landfill to Nassau Lake, in nearby streams and soil, to be removed," she told me.

"I agree," I numbly replied. That outcome seemed more a dream than a possibility.

Trying to think about the EPA and Superfund sites, and frustrations surrounding all of it, I was having a hard time coming up with some key takeaways.

I decided that the best way I could approach these Superfund sites and things I could not see was to think in reverse. Figure out what is not desired and avoid it. It's sometimes known as inversion thinking: avoiding stupidity rather than seeking brilliance.

If we want to eliminate the need for future Superfund sites, the only way forward is to carefully consider any product we make at the design stage. Design with the end in mind so that all by-products of the process can be the feedstock for the same or another process or product.

On my last trip to the lake in the fall, I parked at the southern end and looked out through my car windshield. The road and 30 feet of a grass embankment provided the foreground; yellow, red, green, and brown leaves still on the trees in the distance served as the backdrop. The lake lay in between. A boy cast his line into the lake from the narrow strip of shoreline just in front of where I sat.

He was not a beginner as was demonstrated by his repeated casting ability. Sweeping and well-timed pole motions launched his line far out into the water. The angle of his feet and patience once the line was in the water made me think his casts were finding his intended targets.

I wanted to talk to the boy, but I did not feel comfortable. I am not sure why other than coming across as a strange older guy asking questions. Eventually, I ignored that impulse and got out of the car.

"Catch anything?"

"Not yet," said the boy.

"Do you come here often?"

"I used to live over there." He pointed to the northern side of the lake. "We moved into the village. I like to fish."

The boy's round face was covered above his eyes by hair that was longer on top than the sides and his cheeks were shades of red—a combination of nerves in talking to a stranger, and acne. I spotted a bike lying on the embankment that I assumed was his. The boy was somewhere between 13 and 15 years old.

"I come here when I can. I caught a few yesterday." He was growing more comfortable in talking.

"Did you throw them back?" I responded.

"Yes. You can't take the fish."

"Do you know why?" I asked.

"Something to do with pollution," is all he said. A short, matter-of-fact response. Quick and curt and then he directed his attention back to the task at hand. His shoulders turned to his line in the water. This was also my signal to leave.

"Nice talking. Hope you catch something."

"Thanks," he said.

His reaction to my question echoed the same mantra I experienced at his age: the lake is off limits. I don't want this reaction, this mantra to continue. When the boy is my age, my hope is that the boy he talks to, fishing in the lake, has a story of triumph—that he gets to keep the fish.

Knowing what I don't want is a good step to clarifying what I do want. However, too often, this realization happens too far after recognition. I needed to know what I don't want in anticipation of what may happen, not upon reflection.

To anticipate unintended consequences required thought on multiple levels. Singular linear thinking was not going to provide answers.

Thinking in an anticipatory way, however, might.

Chapter 9

LAKE EFFECTS

The short answer to what happened to the lake is that it was polluted. And that was it. The longer answer is more complete—and more compassionate.

Breaking free of the short answer required a different way of thinking. One where potential outcomes are vetted and invisible effects are exposed. An experience in Cape Cod showed the importance of thinking ahead and understanding all potential consequences.

The wake-up call sounded earlier than normal on vacation. I needed to get my wife, three boys, and the dog into the van by 8:00 a.m. My mental clock had begun as I knew we had a long day ahead. I was also wary of the tide's role in how the day would play out. Tides patterns are affected by gravity, the relative distances and positions of the sun, moon, and Earth, shape of the shoreline, local weather, and wind patterns. In hindsight, I could have paid them more attention.

I'd sold them on the views. I unconsciously or maybe consciously underplayed the effort to get there. We were headed to the Great Island on the Cape Cod National Seashore in Wellfleet, Massachusetts.

We had been vacationing on Cape Cod for the four summers prior but had never ventured this far out on the Cape. Cape Cod is shaped like an arm bent 90 degrees at the elbow. Midway up the inside forearm, the Great Island hangs directly south.

Part of the Cape Cod National Seashore, the Great Island is more accurately a peninsula, as a narrow strip of land connects the island to the mainland. In looking at a map, the land mass almost seems symmetrically out of place—the mainland expands north to Provincetown but the Great Island expands south, sandwiched by Wellfleet Bay and Cape Cod Bay.

The Great Island is shaped like the continent of South America but without Brazil. The missing land is filled by a coastal marsh called the "Gut" that becomes filled with water at high tide.

The main trail begins right off the back edge of the parking lot. The first mile runs along the narrow strip with the Gut to the left as you head south. The early part of the trial trudges through soft sand making every step feel like two. Once past the Gut, the land widens and the trail centers on the land. A rounded hill, hard packed sand, low vegetation, and some small pines cover the interior. A few miles along, the pine forest finally opens to spectacular panoramic views of the connecting bays.

The sun glistened off the choppy waters from all directions and into our squinting eyes. The ocean breeze provided relief to our overheated bodies, and, out of the cover of trees, we felt fresh salty air on our faces. We saw only a handful of people on the hike. Cape Cod beaches and towns are teeming with vacationers in the summer, but this remote place was quiet and untamed. The wind, sun, ocean, and time were the lone ingredients to change. From our elevated view at low tide, a sand bar magically appeared to allow access to another half-mile walk south to the very tip of the land named Jeremy Point.

While the view the tip offered was inviting, the dog's heavy breathing, the sweat on our brows, and our water bottles half empty triggered the decision to go no further. We ate the lunch we had packed on the beach looking across Cape Cod Bay and then headed back. But this time, instead of retracing our steps, we followed a path north along the eastern side of the island.

The beach here looks out to Wellfleet Bay. It is bound by 50-foot-high sand dunes, which acted as a magnet to our kids. To varying degrees of success, all three boys tried to scale the escarpments. My wife and I stayed closer to the water's edge where packed sand made walking easier. We began to trade off who would carry the dog. His small legs were not built for this.

As we approached the Gut, a sinking feeling came over me.

High tide.

The beach ended at the opening of the Gut, which, at low tide, would likely be passable to land on the opposite side about 150 yards away. At high tide, it was not.

Standing in the water in the mouth of the Gut took effort as the rush of incoming water increased in speed and volume. Our oldest saw it as a non-obstacle and began to move forward. He was chest high in water when we quickly re-assessed our options. Our middle child began looking for another path on land. Our youngest stood nervously on the beach. Their instinctive reactions all reflected their different personalities.

Eventually, we found another path on land but it added an hour to our trip. The 9-mile round-trip hike felt like 12 by the time we made it back to the car. Our poor timing, alternate path back, and disregard of tide patterns had added to the adventure but also to our fatigue.

I thought we had a straight path up the east side back to the parking lot. A little deeper thought, some recognition of tide patterns, and clever timing would have questioned that faulty premise and altered our decision-making for the return journey.

The hiking experience made me think about cascading effects. Every decision has second- and third-order effects that are different from the first desired outcome yet trace their roots to the initial decision. The effects are invisible at the time. My decision to leave at the time we did and then to take an alternative route back combined to lead us to a dead end and short of food and water as the time on the trail lengthened.

Similarly, thinking about second- and third-order effects as they apply to Nassau Lake begins to expose the invisible effects.

Nassau Lake had become a friend of sorts. My frequent visits had me rethinking my experiences and memories of it. Thoughts and ideas under my nose for years were too close for me to see. But as I took a step back, beyond the things I saw, there were things I did not see but was becoming more aware existed.

Back in the 1980s, I was a high school student.

One day a student misbehaved. I can't recall what he did, but the teacher sent him out into the hall to sit for a while. I sat in my front row desk and witnessed the brief interaction. Not long after, another adult entered the room. When asked about the student in the hall, the teacher simply whispered "766" by way of explanation.

Now, 766 is the telephone exchange for Nassau. It was the beginning of my phone number growing up and is still the exchange for my parents. The implication seemed to be that the student misbehaved because he was from Nassau. If "766" was common slang, it revealed multiple people reinforcing the underlying implication over many years.

Was this slang term taking a shot at Nassau for being a small village on the edge of the district? A sort of hick town? Was it a socio-economic categorization that provided an easy scapegoat reason for the student's bad behavior? Did the pollution that occurred in the lake decades before now reveal itself in how ill-informed people viewed residents of Nassau? Was it simply a poor-taste joke?

I don't know. I'll never know.

I remember that incident likely because I felt the potential reasons lurked in life's shadows. The pollution seeped into uniformed minds to mislabel a community. A lake with no activity and little investment appears as an easy target to the stereotyping eye for the lake and the surrounding community. It's as if the chemicals rose out of the ground and water to pollinate minds with prejudice and misunderstanding.

I knew that the lake and its reputation were tethered to issues such as housing values, health concerns, biodiversity loss, environmental degradation and mental anguish. But had people ever really seen the connection? Had Nassau always just been misunderstood? How had these issues escaped my attention for 50 years?

I had always viewed the lake through the lens of what I saw as a boy growing up. Like a museum exhibit to observe and move past. I'd compartmentalized it: polluted lake—stay away. This opinion had formed a trench in my mind that blocked my wider understanding of the lake and made my linear thinking easy to justify.

A Yale University course would be the wake-up call I needed to see the bigger picture.

THE BIGGER PICTURE

The executive education course "Corporate Sustainability Management: Risk, Profit, and Purpose" at the Yale School of Management exposed me to a concept referred to as *six capitals* that encapsulate resources needed for a business. These are:

1. Financial—cash assets

2. Manufactured—physical assets

3. Intellectual—knowledge, training, and skills

4. Human—employees and people

5. Social—relationships with and within the community

6. Natural—the environment and biodiversity

Most businesses are focused on the first two. Profitability, cash, total sales, stock price, and asset valuation dominate reporting and goal setting. The other four capitals are equally important but often garner less attention. The sum of these six capitals is the value of a business or economic system.

High profits due to below average labor rates and high environmental degradation is not desirable. Rather than swapping out one capital for another, the goal is to grow all capitals together, because once this is happening consistently, we know we are on the leading edge of sustainability.

I thought of Nassau Lake and the image seared in my mind re-surfaced. Human capital (the girl skiing), natural capital (the lake), and social capital (the lake community) were seemingly disadvantaged for the betterment of financial capital (the truck with barrels dumping waste as a business transaction).

The six capitals are a simplistic model, but they do offer a directional guide to decision-making.

Pollution on a much larger stage can be viewed through the six capitals. As the size of the problem grows, so does the level of complexity. To add to the complexity, the relationship between the capitals changes by region, by industry, and by individual. Not all capitals apply equally, depending on circumstance. Here is an example of one such complexity.

Sachets are a popular packaging solution, particularly in developing countries. Sachets are small, mostly single-serve packets of food (coffee, teas, snacks, spices), medicines, hygiene products (detergents, toothpaste), or conveniences (cigarettes, cell phone cards).

The small size and barrier characteristics which keep the enclosed product fresh provides affordability for people with less means and saves space in smaller households. Single-use sachets also reduce usage volumes, minimize food waste, and lower consumption. Conversely, larger size packages are more prone to waste in the form of spoilage and expiration dates.

When food rots in a landfill environment, it creates methane, which is 20 times more potent a greenhouse gas than carbon dioxide. Food waste costs money, deprives people and harms the planet.[72]

The Philippines has a population of over 100,000 million

people and 23% live below the national poverty line.[73] The small more affordable sachets are an apparent win for human capital. It is also a positive for financial capital for the companies and employees of those companies who produce the products.

However, sachets are a common form of pollution found in oceans. A loss for natural capital.

How does it get there? Many developing countries do not have established waste management systems. The weekly pickups developed countries are used to are largely absent. The result is waste is piled up in the natural environment and swept into rivers by rain, wind, and neglect as more pressing needs take precedence. The waste flows down the rivers and streams and accumulates in the ocean. The ocean acts as a sink for waste that falls outside of any waste management system that may exist.

The Philippines is an archipelago in the Western Pacific Ocean consisting of more than 7,000 islands. Sachets are sold in most developing countries, but the number sold in the Philippines is astonishing—163 million sachets a day or 60 billion a year. Data from the Department for Environment and Natural Resources (DENR) shows that a five-day coastal clean-up on Freedom Island in Manila Bay in the Philippines in August 2019 produced a total of 16,000 kg (35,000 pounds) of trash.[74]

The reliance on sachets for an island nation with limited waste management systems combines to hit the ocean pollution bullseye.

While not perfect, there are solutions which will begin to build human, financial, and natural capital together. Growing all three simultaneously provides people necessary nutrition, hygiene, and medicines and keeps packaging out of the natural environment in a financially viable way.

Designing sachet packages for recyclability or composting, investment in waste management infrastructure, raising incomes to allow for buying in greater quantities, moving toward reusable packaging business models, involving producers in the responsibility to collect packages they produce at the-of-life, and labeling packaging with end-of-life options all offer alternatives to positively affect multiple capitals at once instead of sacrificing one for another.

Interactions and tradeoffs occur across all industries. The examples are countless, the relationships are endless, and effects are limitless. Wrapping our heads around solutions to all these at once is impossible. Thinking about them beyond the initial premise is not.

Going beyond first-order thinking helps to find solutions that provide maximum benefit. First-order thought focuses on what appears to be the immediate result of taking an action. We see the sachets in the ocean and want to stop making them. Second-order thinking knows stopping the production of sachets abruptly may in turn affect the hygiene, health, and well-being of people reliant on them, at least in the short term. Third-order thinking begins to look at the implications of malnutrition and lack of medical care.

For Nassau Lake, the second- and third-order effects of dumping in the landfill were either not considered important enough to care for, were not fully understood, or more likely were a complex combination of both. Dumping waste in open pits was common at the time yet since realization hit that the waste was causing damage, progress toward resolution and clean-up has been painfully slow. The layered effects are still being felt.

Dave Fleming is the Nassau town supervisor and has held the position for more than a decade. Dave grew up in the northeastern part of the town. His interest in the lake and politics began in the 1990s.

I went to the Town of Nassau offices in January of 2022 to talk to Dave. The historic building sits on Church Street just a three-minute walk from the main intersection in Nassau. I had seen this building in photographs I found at the Nassau Public Library archives from 200-plus years ago. It looks the same today. I had also passed the building in a car, on a bike, or on foot thousands of times as a kid and as an adult but had never visited.

I met Dave in his office on the second floor. We talked for about 45 minutes.

I asked why it took so long to act on the contamination of the landfill, the lake, and the surrounding area.

"The solution to pollution is dilution," Dave said.

Well, that was a jolt to my brain. I'd just found a connection between Nassau and Picher, Oklahoma. In short, the government would let the chemicals settle and over time they would dissipate. I began to believe the 1,300-plus Superfund sites experienced the same response of inaction as the Superfund football gets kicked from one political regime to the next.

"Is the contamination issue a social justice issue?" I asked.

"It's an economic, health, and social generational issue," Dave said.

He went further, telling me a story of a woman who lives close to the lake whom he had visited when campaigning. She was brought to tears talking about the contamination and its effect on her life.

"People having water filtration systems in their homes for

years for drinking water is not right," Dave told me. "I wish people knew that this issue affects us all."

He went on to say that those close to the site are not the only ones affected. People within the town pay more taxes to compensate for those with homes closer to the site who get tax breaks.

Dave mentioned the town's work on public preserves and nature trails. Stewart Preserve, Albert Family Community Forest, Kinderhook Creek Preserve, and Mud Pond Preserve are four of the growing number of public lands in the town of Nassau. The marketing pamphlet states, "The Town of Nassau is filled with rugged natural beauty and public spaces and is a gateway to the Rensselaer Plateau."

These nature trails combine with the new bike trail that follows the former 28-mile train line. The railways were removed, and pavement laid in their place. The bike trail runs tangent to the southern end of the lake and tracks through the heart of Nassau.

Dave was proud of the town's work to now have more than 650 acres of public space of varying ecosystems to explore and was excited to see activity on the bike trail.

"They help offset the 'lake effect'," he said.

I knew what he meant. The public lands are a potential attraction for visitors. The new recreational opportunities hope to chip away at and erode the instinct to stay away.

Dave has a passion for the lake and the town. He is an eloquent speaker, steadfast and professional in his approach. Nassau is lucky to have him.

My last question to Dave was, what is the next step in helping the lake?

"Containment," he said. "The landfill is not completely sealed. Contamination still leaks out particularly in times of heavy rainfall."

This was not the first time I had heard this. Barbara Reina had mentioned it, too.

The comment was disheartening. Sixty years later and the toxic chemicals are still leaking.

I walked away thinking the businesses that created the contamination and the government's role in holding people accountable and acting on behalf of the community has been a 60-year hot potato. The potato is passed from politician to politician and generation to generation as funding for clean-up, accurate information to encapsulate the issue, and political will to make it all happen are a multi-focus lens that has, to date, been unable to focus on the same vision of a solution.

Our talk exposed politics as a potential obstacle to people finding their sustainability boats. Another ski-masked thief to steal a sustainability mindset. Without the right laws and regulations, short-term goals trump long-term sustainability efforts. Without the political will, efforts are slowed and weighed down, like swimming with clothes on, walking in quicksand, or biking with a flat tire.

Second- and third-order thinking helps us see what is not easily seen. The invisible becomes more obvious, leading to better choices, and in turn better choices are aided by better information.

I needed better information.

Chapter 10

IGNORANCE IS NO EXCUSE

gnorance was a shield for me as a kid. It offered protection. Because I was young, no one challenged me to know more, and I didn't feel a responsibility to either. I was comfortable then not knowing, or at least pretending not to.

That changed one afternoon as a 13-year-old.

The house I grew up in was midway down Elm Street. Streetlights, fully mature trees, and sidewalks guarded the quarter mile pavement. The road ran straight from the sole traffic light in the middle of the village to a split—each road led to opposite sides of the lake a few miles north. The old homes were built close together and all just five to 10 steps off the sidewalk. The proximity of the front porches to the street allowed for easy conversation with neighbors and passersby.

Behind the row of houses across the street was a downslope that led to a large swamp. The forested wetland extended the length of the street and went out as far as my 13-year-old eyes could see. From an early age, I knew to stay out of the swamp for two reasons.

The first reason was snakes. The swamp was saturated with them—mostly garter snakes, but it was easy to be convinced of larger and more dangerous ones lurking in the tall weeds and murky water.

Second were the rumors that people had died in the swamp. As a kid, I likely fanned the flames of those rumors by re-telling stories of unidentified people from the distant past getting caught or worse, dragged under the black water, never to be seen again, especially after heavy rains when the swamp swelled to twice its normal size. I had no evidence of this but also heard no objections to the stories from my group of friends.

One spring day after days of rain, the swamp water ballooned to almost three times its normal volume. The small random out-croppings that normally appeared as tiny islands peppering the swamp were fully submerged. A few smaller trees poked through the water's surface marking their now invisible base. The speed of the water's flow had increased as much as the volume. That is what caught our attention.

My two neighbors and I stared at the rushing water. With a mix of hubris and excitement, the three of us quickly pulled a canoe off the shed behind my house before we could reconsider. We dropped the canoe into the water, and the current whisked us away from shore. We were all exploring the swamp for the first time. Turbulent water snatched silt from the bottom to form a brown cocktail of dirt preventing us from seeing more than a few inches below the surface. The dark waters fed into the chilling rumors. We were afraid of what lay beneath the surface, but we were moving too fast to give it much thought. We knew the water would eventually lead to a bridge at the edge of town.

The channel narrowed as it fed into the chokepoint under the bridge. As it did, the water flowed faster. From a distance, we could see that our canoe would not make it under the bridge—the water level was too high. But then we noticed a bigger problem.

My mom. Two hands clenched to the bridge rails, her body rigid, she was staring straight at us. She had magically pieced together the missing canoe, missing son, and missing neighbors in short order and cut us off at the outskirts of the village.

The racing current carried us toward her. I hastily prepared my excuse. My mind toggled between not knowing the danger and my friends forcing my hand. Both were untrue. I could not pick up the shield of ignorance now. Fortunately, we were able to pull off to the side and get home safely. I did not see my friends for a week—they were grounded just like me.

I don't recall my parents ever being more disappointed in me than that day. I knew better. I knew it was dangerous. I knew the risks. I chose short-term, selfish pleasure over recognizing obvious peril.

Pleading ignorance was no excuse.

Though it's still tempting to pick that shield back up on occasion, I find it a less appealing defense as more time passes. Ignorance no longer seems like a form of protection—instead, it's a great obstacle. Not knowing presents a challenge. A challenge to find information from multiple sources to form an opinion. An opinion not to impress upon others but rather to enable you to participate and add to the dialogue.

I had been shielding myself from the truth about Nassau Lake and the issues surrounding climate for decades. But this was no longer acceptable. I lowered the shield. It was my responsibility to know—and to do something with that knowledge.

I began to see Nassau Lake as a microcosm of climate change.

I became despondent at the traditional cliched sustainability narrative parroting the command to reduce, reuse, and recycle. How could we go beyond that?

There are eight factors that have re-framed how I think about climate change and Nassau Lake.

1. Life Cycle Analysis: In general, Life Cycle Analysis or LCA attempts to provide an objective, scientific measure to assess the environmental impacts associated with various stages of a product's life cycle: sourcing, manufacturing, distribution, use, and recovery. Measurements are taken at each stage and combined to provide a total impact.

By example, a loaf of bread on the store shelf is typically found in a package with a hard plastic closure. The saleable product's LCA would measure the package and the bread enclosed. The environmental impacts of water use, air pollution, energy use, GHG emissions, mineral use, and chemical toxicity would be looked at for every ingredient in the bread, the package, and the closure in every stage of the product's life. The complexity grows when the same analysis of the impacts and stages is done for the "ingredients of the ingredients"—where is the flour made, how is it made, the transport distance to the flour-making plant, etc. The more ingredients, the more complex. Where does the analysis end?

Most LCAs will use proxies or estimates for some of the analysis. LCAs are approximations attempting to consolidate the data into a single number that represents the whole complex life cycle. As environmental impacts are better known and more data is gathered, more robust data can be pooled, and ultimately better approximations can be made.

The hope is one day, we will see an LCA label that is both simple to understand yet accurate to the complexity it represents. LCA labels inform consumers and allow them to buy more easily based on environmental impacts. Brands will respond to consumer demand and in doing so, the negative impacts will be more easily avoided. If brands are incentivized for lower environmental impact because of having to label their products to appeal to consumers, it will drive the market toward circularity.

Every product made has a shadow that spans its entire life cycle from creation to disposal. The darkness and reach of the shadow is exposed by an accurate LCA. The aim is an acceptable level of welfare without creating future environmental problems.

2. Top down and Bottom Up: Termites. Most of these creatures are blind. Individually, they wander aimlessly. However, if enough termites come together in the right conditions, they become formidable architects. The queen communicates from the top and the workers respond from the bottom to build extraordinary mounds that can grow to 100 feet around and 25 feet tall.

The "top-down" approach comes from government policies and mandates. Climate is not a singular problem. It has multiple causes and causes multiple issues. It is hard to govern around things that don't have a singular cause. In a top-down approach, system level changes force action amongst businesses and individuals. The top-down approach can be a slow process as it requires aligning the interests of a wide variety of groups around a probably imperfect policy.

The "bottom-up" approach focuses on individual actions. It requires individuals to change their own behavior in the hope of influencing policy. Bottom-up strategies can be quicker to move, but they tend to have less impact.

The history of the landfill and Nassau Lake clean-up efforts shows a combination of both top-down and bottom-up approaches.

<u>Top Down:</u> In 1968, the Loeffel Waste Oil and Service Company operating at the landfill was ordered to stop discharging waste from the facility and perform remedial activities by a New York Supreme Court Order and Judgment against the company.[75]

The judgment was in response to numerous complaints from the community including dead fish, water "unsuitable" for agriculture, "acrid smoke" from materials being burned, and concerns over "seepage into shallow wells." These complaints accumulated over time and can be found in articles under headlines like "Air, Stream Pollution Being Probed" April 15, 1965 from the *Times Record*[76] and "Nassau Co. Cited in Oil Polluting" from *The Record*, May 5, 1966.[77]

The Nassau landfill was not alone. "Troy Feels 'Pure Water' Whip" was the front-page headline in the *Troy Record* September 2, 1965. The article goes into detail about how citizens' increasing concern over gross pollution of the state's waters. "As was emphasized by the state health leaders, the entire Hudson River Valley, particularly in the capital district, is highly polluted." Nassau resides in the Hudson Valley—this was clearly a widespread problem. [78]

New York State Department of Environmental Conservation (NYSDEC) and companies identified as responsible for the contamination (General Electric, Schenectady Chemical, and Bendix) performed numerous investigations and clean-up actions under the NYSDEC's Superfund program from 1980 until EPA added the site to the federal NPL Superfund sites in March 2011.

Activities included installing a clay cap to the landfill, adding a "soil/bentonite clay slurry" wall at the landfill to limit the chemicals from escaping, monitoring, and maintaining residential well treatment systems, and removing contamination off site.

Since 2013, groundwater has been collected and treated on-site using a water treatment plant. The system is designed to extract contamination such as VOCs, PCBs, and 1,4-dioxane from the groundwater before it is discharged into a nearby stream.[79] Regular sampling of the treated water is an ongoing process.

<u>Bottom Up:</u> Three groups in Nassau have existed or been formed over the years to protect the lake and/or participate in the clean-up process.

Nassau Lake Park Improvement Association (NLPIA). Established in 1925, the organization serves as the gatekeeper for access to the lake. Permits are issued for a small fee on an annual basis. The NLPIA also organizes different events and committees surrounding clean-up efforts. I became a member in 2020 to have access to boating on the lake.

CAG (Community Advisory Group). A CAG is a committee or task force of community and government stakeholders that meet to discuss and gather updates about the contaminated site. I joined the CAG calls in 2021

UNCAGED (United Neighbors Concerned About General Electric and the Dewey Loeffel Landfill) has been advocating for the total clean-up of the landfill and surrounding areas including Nassau Lake since 2000. The heads of the organization for many years were Kelly Travers Main and Pam Lever. I connected with Kelly on the phone to learn more about their work.

Kelly described UNCAGED as a grassroots, passionate group

of people who aim to move faster and to stand up to government agencies to hold them accountable.

I asked her, "What do you mean 'move faster'?"

"Be like a chihuahua biting at the ankles of the government," she said, "[to get them] to do what they said they would do."

"What did they say they would do?" I asked.

"Contain the waste and then set a plan to remove it," she replied.

There was that word again: contain. I had heard "containment" as a primary issue now from multiple people and sources.

"Our group kept telling the government that they 'need to go higher and deeper'," Kelly said.

"Higher up, closer to the landfill, and deeper where the underground movement of chemicals is likely occurring."

Kelly relayed that the group's focus on the source was in response to the New York State government finding chemicals downhill and downstream from the landfill in the 1990s and "families getting sick from their water."

UNCAGED was mostly active until the federal government EPA program took over in 2012 and conducted interviews to form the CAG. The CAG includes local elected officials, EPA representatives, and community members. UNCAGED advocated with and helped bring the CAG group up to speed.

Kelly is a member of the CAG group but has slowed her activism. "CAG is a government group," Kelly said with some reluctance. I could tell from our conversation her passions for the lake lie with the grassroots group who challenged the government for faster movement.

I asked Kelly how she sees this playing out.

"I do not see it getting better—it's likely to end up as a swamp. My fear is the government does not see it as a natural lake, which it isn't—it is a dammed-up creek. Jonathan Hoag created the lake years ago to provide power to mills closer to the village." The inference was that distinction may not give the lake, the landfill, and surrounding areas the full attention it needs for a total clean-up for future generations.

I thanked Kelly for her work and dedication over the many years. Her activism was inspiring—acting on behalf of the lake even when resulting actions to clean up were delayed, slowed, or seemingly stopped all together.

From a top-down approach, finally getting on the federal list of Superfund sites in 2011 provides a better chance of securing the resources necessary to clean up the landfill, lake, and surrounding area. Meanwhile, the bottom-up organizations continue to work for more immediate change.

Termites seem to leverage the best of both approaches. Individual termites know their roles with some communication from the queen to construct large homes that can last hundreds of years. The aim of the best sustainability movements is to do the same: a centralized approach creating governmental policies in alignment with reasonable business goals and individual actions.

3. Safe and Circular. The Toxic Substance Control Act (TSCA) of 1976 gives the EPA the authority to require reporting, record-keeping, and testing requirements and restrictions related to chemical substances. Chemicals used are meant to be safe and circular. Circular meaning they are reusable, recyclable, or compostable at the end of life.

There are over 80,000 chemicals on the market in the United States. The EPA has banned five of those that were around before the Act went into effect. These include:

PCBs: PCBs were used in hundreds of industrial and commercial applications. These are toxic to humans, animals, and some plants.

Fully Halogenated Chlorofluorocarbons: A predominant component of aerosol sprays until ozone depletion was discovered as a major problem. Ozone in the atmosphere shields us from harmful UV rays that can cause skin cancer.

Dioxins: A harmful class of toxic chemical compounds. One of the worst applications was the use of a dioxin as an ingredient in Agent Orange—a herbicide used by the United States in the Vietnam War to expose the forest areas that might conceal the enemy. Dioxins in high quantities can cause cancer and are linked to reproductive, developmental, and immune system issues.

Asbestos: Widely used for insulation and in the construction of cars and ships. The tiny asbestos fibers can get caught in lungs and can cause cancer over time.

Hexavalent Chromium: Used as paint for cars, boats, and planes since it creates hard metal coatings. The chemical can cause cancer. [80]

The purposes and products the banned chemicals served have now, in large part, been replaced by safer chemicals. Chemicals that are less toxic, and more circular at the end of their usable life.

But prior to 1976 these noxious chemicals were widely used, seemingly without anyone knowing their full, enduring, and damaging effect.

Nassau Lake is the effect. When was it known that PCBs dumped in open pits would cause harmful generational effects? And when was that knowledge acted upon? The longer the gap between knowing and acting, the more damage is caused. Determining the extent of the time gap for Nassau Lake was not going to be easy.

4. Environmental Social Governance. Environmental Social Governance (ESG) offers a framework to evaluate a business's sustainability and ethical impact.

The Financial Accounting Standards Board or FASB was founded in 1973 and established financial accounting and reporting standards for public and private companies that follow Generally Accepted Accounting Principles (GAAP). These standards are now well established. Many organizations are now seeking to standardize sustainability reporting in the same way.

The Sustainability Accounting Standards Board or SASB is one organization trying to set reporting standards on non-financial factors for better transparency on material risks and growth opportunities. SASB seeks to set standards for environmental, social and governance criteria for companies.

Standardized reporting on businesses' non-monetary issues includes greenhouse gas emissions, water use, sustainable sourcing, fairness in the workplace, inclusivity, employee turnover, corporate giving, impact investing, board diversity, company oversight, air quality, community involvement, and waste reduction. The list of areas covered is extensive. Transparent reporting across the board will allow investors and consumers to make decisions to support business based on a holistic knowledge of that business.

A poor ESG report can make a more profitable company less attractive to investors and consumers. The reverse is also true—a less profitable company may be more attractive due to its high ESG performance. It's hard to improve what is not measured. SASB and other organizations like it are striving to make ESG reporting standard practice.

5. Prepare for the exponential. It is easier for most to think about "linear" relationship graphs that tilt up or down in a straight line depending on the relationship between two variables. For example, businesses will experiment with price to see how it affects sales. Slight increases or decreases in price will likely impact the sales in incremental amounts.

Exponential graphs are harder to comprehend. An exponential graph is like a Nike swoosh rotated 90 degrees. The steep curved lines of exponential graphs reveal the rapid increase or decrease of a variable in relation to small changes in another. The relationship between time and CO_2 emissions follows an exponential growth graph. In 1850, the world's annual CO_2 emissions from fossil fuels stood at 196 million tons. By 1900, the number had grown to 1.9 billion tons. In 1950, 6 billion. In 2000, 25 billion. In 2020, 35 billion.[81]

The time–CO_2 emissions graph looks like an ever-rising Olympic ski jump hill. We are presently at the top, but looking up instead of down.

If we can anticipate where exponential growth may occur,

we can better prepare for or avoid the potential impact. Without forecasting, we are stuck with rapid and extreme consequences.[82]

6. Warming Basics and Statistics. The sun's solar radiation in the form of light waves passes through the Earth's atmosphere. Most of the radiation is absorbed to warm the Earth while some energy is reflected back into space in the form of infrared rays. As CO_2 concentration increases, more and more outgoing infrared is trapped in the atmosphere: this is global warming.

In 2020, humans emitted approximately 35 billion tons of CO_2 into the thin shell of the atmosphere by burning fossil fuels. That would cover 915,000 square miles—almost the equivalent of completely covering Texas and Alaska.[83]

Each year adds more CO_2, resulting in more warming. The seven hottest years on record are from 2013 to 2020. Nineteen of the hottest 20 are between 2000 and 2020.[84] The same extra heat that evaporates more water from the ocean causes bigger downpours, and more intense storms and floods pull moisture even more quickly out of the soil causing longer and deeper droughts and higher potential for fire. Worldwide weather-related catastrophes have quadrupled in cost since 1980.[85]

7. Keeping an Open Mind. My mantra about Nassau Lake has always been naively simple: Stay out. Stay out turned into stay away. This journey and the people I have met has changed that mantra.

Kurt Vincent, Barbara Reina, Kelly Maine Travers, and Dave Fleming have not stayed away. They have written about, met about, spoken on behalf of, or fought for the lake for years. The direction toward improvement is what has grown to be most important even if all the answers are not yet available.

Being more open-minded has also changed my view of how to think about climate change. While I believe in renewable resource use at creation and a defined end of life with no waste as a goal, I am increasingly aware of solutions that do not fit this exactly but offer a more circular solution than the current state. Progress has to be the goal as there are no absolute answers. Being closed-minded to directionally better solutions is a villain sneaking up to take access away from sustainability boats.

The continuing use of landfill as a destination for waste offers an example. Landfills are essentially tombs. With no oxygen to aid breakdown, methane is released as a by-product and gains an invite to the atmospheric party of greenhouse gases. Methane is a far more potent greenhouse gas than CO2. Landfill is not the end-of-life goal for waste. That said, more than 50% of waste in the United States ends up in landfill. Methane is essentially a natural gas. The EPA tracks more than 2,600 municipal solid waste land-fills. About 500 collect methane to produce energy while about 500 more could collect the gas at a reasonable cost. Capturing it to be used for energy closes a loop and represents better circular flow than methane released into the environment.[86]

Being more open-minded is tied to progress, not perfection.

8. Front Line and Fence Line Communities: Front line communities are those that experience environmental impacts of climate change first-hand. For example, a subsistence farmer feels the direct effects of higher variations in weather patterns. More floods and droughts make farming less productive and survival less certain.

Fence line communities feel the direct effects of living or working next to industrial sites, disposal areas, and company operations that neglect the negative externalities of the entity. In simple terms, externalities arise when a company takes action but does not bear all the costs of that action.

For years, some companies have treated the environment as an externality. The environment is too often not viewed as a stakeholder to whom corporations need to pay attention. Negative externalities reveal themselves in a variety of forms—deteriorating public health, climate change, natural resource depletion, and biodiversity loss are just a few. If the environment is treated as a stakeholder, those externalities become internal costs to the company. The range of impacts are wide—polluted air, water, and land, noise, mental and physical health concerns, economic devaluation, and even survival.

Fence line and front line communities take many forms. Think of small island communities that are forced to move due to rising sea levels. Think neighborhoods living next to a dump site that emits hazardous gasses. Think of communities around larger manufacturers that pollute air, land, and water. Think about the family who cannot afford to buy an air conditioner when the temperature and humidity rise to unprecedented levels.

According to the National Center for Environmental Information in July of 2022, a deadly heat wave set or tied 359 daily high temperature records along with 709 records for the warmest overnight low temperature.[87] The 709 number caught my attention. My small upstairs bedroom growing up was in the back left corner of our house. We did not have air conditioning. On hot summer days, temperatures dropping with the sun and a small fan in my bedroom window offered the primary hope of a decent night's sleep. There were a few nights where the high temperature relegated the fan to merely a noise maker. With hot air blowing, I lay awake on top of my sheets, sweat forming from the slightest movement. Record nighttime highs mean more sleepless nights for more people.

The climate issue is a social justice issue. The results of climate change have a much higher and disproportionate effect on those groups of people who have contributed least to the problem —low income and marginalized populations. Addressing both climate and social justice allows progress on both.

The EPA Superfund website states, "while there is no single way to characterize communities located near our sites, the population is more minority, more lower-income, linguistically isolated, and less likely to have a high school education than the US population as a whole."[88] Those with less are burdened with more.

The sum of these eight factors moves beyond reduce, reuse, and recycle. They expose a few first-order principles. First-order principles are the foundational elements of understanding—the original principles from which other things are deduced. For example, the rules of a sport govern what can and cannot be done. The rules are the foundational element of the game. They are truisms that are not challenged.

FIRST-ORDER PRINCIPLES

Three key understandings came to be, in my mind, first-order principles.

- Increasing levels of CO2 in the environment warm the planet

- Preservation of the environment is essential to long-term survival

- The climate issue is a social justice issue

If we take a short-term view, and don't adopt these principles, we will never get into the sustainability boat. If, however, we take a long-term approach and believe these principles, getting into the boat becomes natural. To consistently choose to not get in your sustainability boat without any regard to preservation will eventually lead to a dead end—the planet will survive but we as humans will be less equipped to survive on it.

If taking the long-term view seems unattainable, how then to get people to make repeated short-term decisions to get into the boat? I know there is no silver bullet to this as I have fallen out of my boat many times. That seems unavoidable to me—the short-term decision will always attract traffic. But once I began to accept the existence of the short-term instinct, I concentrated on what it would take to get back in the boat once out. What gets us back on the fairway when we hit our ball in the short-term ruff?

So far, I had found a lot of reasons to compel people to get into their sustainability boats. Connection to others, community, path dependence, circular systems, personal actions, guilt, knowing the Earth's resources are finite, a growing oversight by lawmakers, six capitals thinking, inversion, second- and third-order effects and first order principles are all motivations.

However, the band of thieves forming to steal a sustainability mindset is growing fast. Pure ownership mentality that ignores the common good, a 'not in my backyard' philosophy, selfishness, the notion that individual actions seem inconsequential, pleading ignorance, convenience, cost, apathy, lack of political will, closed-mindedness, short-term survival, and taking the path of least resistance were challenges to which I had no immediate counter-argument. To dissuade the instinct to continue business as usual. To turn apathetic minds from thinking "it's not a big deal" or that "we've got time." To make them want to get into their boat.

I began to question what I was doing. My efforts were convincing me to get out of my boat instead of encouraging others to get into theirs.

Chapter 11

UP IN SMOKE

My growing frustration to find answers brought up a Nassau experience long ago deposited in my memory bank. Up until that point, my hometown had seemed immune to catastrophe. My innocence was about to change forever.

In early July of 1982, I stood and looked out at the flag waving above the scoreboard in centerfield. My dad stood next to me just as he had for so many years. He was my coach. My Nassau Little League baseball team was finishing our season. Unfortunately, the game intersected with our Vermont family vacation. Dad and I came home to play the game and then headed two hours north back up to camp. This game was different.

On this particular July night, the humidity sat on all of us. Any movement required a sacrifice of sweat to cut through the thick air. The sun began to drop but the lingering effects of the summer sun did not fade quickly. As we took infield in our home park prior to the game, the haze left over from the day seemed thicker than normal. The hot fog typically lightened as day became evening but that night, it got worse. Added to the heavy air was a scent of smoke. The smell grew stronger.

Prior to every game, our team would line up on the first base baseline and look at the raised flag beyond the outfield fence. A recorded, static-laden rendition of the national anthem would blare over the loudspeaker.

I looked out just as I had for the 50-plus games I had played in the four years prior. I had to squint to see the flag. The smoke had become so thick, the flag was mostly hidden from view. The strong smell of smoke diverted my attention to what we were all thinking.

Fire trucks, sirens, police lights, and commotion powered through the humidity and smoke-filled air. I thought for sure that the game would be canceled but it was not. The smoke subsided. We eventually carried on and played the game, but the result was dropped from my memory long ago.

Delson's department store burned to the ground that night—it was arson. A block away from the Little League field and two blocks from my house, Delson's was the place in town to buy anything. A hula hoop, some nails, a cantaloupe, a window screen, some baseball cards, and everything in between—you could get it all at Delson's. The store was a constant in Nassau since it opened in 1910.

After the game, my dad and I walked to the scene. The fire was mostly extinguished by then. Smoke continued to escape from the charred wreckage and the smell of wet wood and doused flames grew stronger as we approached the smoldering store. A snake pit of fire hoses filled the street in front. The urgency to contain the blaze required help from adjacent town fire departments—more than 15 responded. Red and yellow fire trucks were strewn in front of the building and along all adjoining streets. It seemed everyone from Nassau was there. A stunned, silent crowd. The looks on the gathered faces was something my 12-year-old eyes had never seen before.

Disbelief, shock, and tears dominated. I stood next to my dad feeling a little of each. I am glad I was with my dad that night, and with so many people from Nassau, but I still felt alone as I knew every person there was feeling his or her own way through what we were witnessing.

I looked at the smoke as it separated from its source. I watched it as it rose. Black then thinning to gray, then disappearing into the evening sky.

Delson's was gone.

The more I searched for reasons to get into my sustainability boat, the less belief I had that I would succeed in helping other people into theirs. Instead of uncovering new paths for moving forward, I was revealing obstacles that were much larger than I'd thought, while exposing dated personal scars of guilt and inaction. Each revelation was a body blow to my efforts, my psyche, and my goal. Delson's was gone and so was my motivation to keep going.

The obstacles crushing my motivation boiled down to the existence of three things that seemed to define the journey. Without acknowledging and resolving them, my journey to sustainability and hope of helping others, once as solid as Delson's, would burn to the ground.

1. PCBs Polychlorinated biphenyls or PCBs are the primary chemicals in the lake. Earlier, we found out that PCBs were used for a wide range of everyday applications. The plethora of uses in the 1900s led to mass production.

To date between 1 and 1.5 million tons of PCBs have been produced worldwide with only 17% being eliminated. PCBs tend to remain attached to soils or sediments so any process which moves soils or sediments, also moves the chemicals.

They can easily cycle between air, water, and soil. PCBs can also evaporate from water or soil and be carried long distances to areas far away from the original release point. Consequently, they are found all over the world.

PCBs are so prevalent in the world, "everyone in the world is likely to have PCB quantities in his or her body."[89]

I began to think of PCBs' dispersal like dropping a hundred handfuls of tiny round beads. Once dropped, the beads scatter, whereby retrieval of each is almost impossible. Add in wind and water that blows and flows at various rates, and the spread gets exponentially worse. I began to understand why clean-ups are so complicated.

PCBs are not just in the lake. The waterways that lead from the landfill to the lake are also contaminated. The shallow streams are narrow at times and swell with storms. When sediments move, so do PCBs. With little chance to settle to the bottom of shallow water and due to the changing widths of stream beds, PCBs move in various directions with each storm. Testing a stream bank to find PCBs one year and testing the same area the next and not finding the same result is not uncommon.

They are a moving target—the scale of the clean-up needed is massive.

"Wells Contaminated in Nassau From State Superfund Site" was the headline in the *Times Union* newspaper on December 7, 2021. "Trucks that hauled loads to the Dewey Loeffel Landfill are believed to have gone to the site on Route 203 to be washed out, resulting in contamination." The article went on to say, "it's going south toward Columbia County,"—"it" meaning toxic chemicals, including PCBs.[90]

The article is from 2021. Not 1971.

Contaminated water flows into the Valatie Kill stream, which in turn feeds Nassau Lake. The lake is dammed at the southern end where the overflowing water re-feeds the Valatie Kill and continues flowing toward Nassau Village. The Valatie Kill continues its march south, running alongside Route 203. The property along Route 203 is near the Valatie Kill about a mile south of the village.

A landfill federal Superfund site north of the village and a residential property New York State Superfund site to the south. The village is in a Superfund sandwich.

The already open wound grows.

2. Microplastics Microplastics are plastic particles less than 5 millimeters (0.2 inches) in diameter—about the size of a popcorn kernel. There are two categories of microplastics: primary and secondary.

Primary microplastics are designed for commercial use—cosmetics, microfibers shed from clothing, fishing nets, etc. Secondary microplastics are particles that result from the breakdown of larger plastic items such as water bottles, bags, and utensils. Sun radiation and ocean waves are the main factors in breaking them down.[91]

About 98% of microplastics come from land use meaning they are created on land and enter waterways, eventually finding their way to the ocean. About 63% of microplastics are estimated to stem from two sources. Firstly, the laundering of synthetic textiles. Laundering creates microplastics through the shedding of fibers and these fibers, like polyester, are discharged into sewer systems and potentially wind up in the ocean. Secondly, the abrasion of tires. Tires consist of natural rubber and a mix of synthetic polymers. When being used in driving they erode and this synthetic rubber is carried away by wind or washed off the road by rain.

The remaining 37% of particles come from a wide variety of sources—personal care items (cosmetics), detergents, marine coatings, road markings, plastic pellet loss (pellets are melted to make plastics), artificial turf, building coatings, and plastic packaging. Plastic packaging—that's me.[92]

Like PCBs, the problem with microplastics is that they do not readily break down. Plastics can take hundreds of years to decompose. Plastic's superior strength as a material for use is also its biggest weakness at end of life if treated as disposable.

According to *Nature* magazine's May 2021 article, "Microplastics are everywhere but are they harmful?"[93] scientists have "seen microplastics everywhere they have looked: in deep oceans, in Arctic snow and Antarctic ice, in shellfish, table salt, drinking water and beer." The article goes on to say, "from limited surveys of microplastics in the air, water, salt, and seafood, children and adults might ingest anywhere from dozens to more than 100,000 microplastic specks each day."

The microplastic issue is not going away—plastics production is expected to double by 2050.

I began to think about how we at our manufacturing facility dispose of plastic waste. We create over 250 tons of plastic waste per year in making custom packaging. We have consistently captured over 99% of internal waste and recycled it through commercial recycling plants. The waste is used to make a wide variety of items—more packaging, fence posts, decking, carpets, etc. Waste from a manufacturing facility like ours is sought after as it is not "contaminated" as it would be in a consumer waste stream.

My father owned our family business along with my grandfather back in the 1960s. I wondered what they did with the waste back then, when there were no recycling systems in place.

I cringed before I asked my dad this question. I already knew the answer.

"The dump. It was the only means of disposal prior to recycling infrastructure being built," he responded.

I knew if we went to that dump, we would likely be able to find that waste plastic under mounds of earth. The prospect of doing so was paralyzing.

3. Unchecked Consumerism *Doublethink* is accepting two contradictory thoughts simultaneously and accepting them both as correct. Holding two opposing thoughts in the mind at the same time and making sense out of each. George Orwell's *1984* exposed me to the concept.

"War is peace" is one of the doublethink slogans in the book. In other words, war overseas provides a common enemy to protect the peace at home. This seems to have some logic to it. The logic wanes, however, when you realize it is not clear there is a war being fought in the book.

The "Party" or government has propagandized the war to keep people united. With attention focused elsewhere, the Party can prevent people from becoming consciously aware of the obvious problems at home. It's easier for the Party to rule with a common enemy overseas. Multiple other examples of doublethink define the book.

I wondered if there was a correlation between doublethink and climate.

Something like Consumerism is Preservation.

Economic growth is one of the top priorities of governments. Growth drives policy and messaging. The messaging seems to indicate that if we are not growing, we are dying. In order to preserve our economy, we need to consume. Companies drive to sell more to meet quarterly projections, and, to satisfy shareholders, combine to form a monster of consumerism in a condensed time frame. Short-term results matter most in an economy where 70% represents the consumer-spending portion of Gross Domestic Product.[94]

It seems that every commercial, social media post, billboard, text, or email from a company is trying to get us to consume. Buy things to grow the economy. What we do not get is a link to the effects of our consumerism on climate—when we buy more, we generally use more resources and create more emissions. But if the economy is good, people are happy. Consumerism is the shiny object that holds our attention while the Earth is the hidden sacrifice.

Incentives to preserve are backwards. GDP grows when we cut down a tree or extract raw materials to make things. It does not grow when we plant a tree or keep from using materials.

An economy based on less carbon, managing materials that already exist, and more circular and serviced-based business models does not garner much attention yet offers a way to keep consuming as we wish while holding the environment as a key stakeholder.

War is peace. Consumerism is preservation.

I have been in consumer doublethink mode my whole life.

THE LINK

"A Growing Toxic Threat—Made Worse by Climate Change" was the headline from *Inside Climate News* on September 24, 2020.[95] Hurricanes, floods, and wildfires are bad news for toxic waste sites. When natural disasters hit these sites, the contained chemicals have an increased chance of escape.

The San Jacinto River offers an example. Dioxins, a now banned chemical by the EPA, was dumped in and around the San Jacinto River near Houston by paper mills in the 1960s. The responsible parties installed a temporary cap over the waste on the Superfund site under the guidance of the EPA. Hurricane Harvey hit in 2017 causing heavy damage to the cap resulting in high levels of dioxins being detected in the surrounding area.[96]

Nassau has experienced the same problem caused by natural events. "Water Pollution Fears Linger" was the headline in the *Times Union* newspaper on August 3, 2021. The article stated that historic flooding on July 14, 2021 made it clear that damage was done to areas around the Dewey Loeffel Superfund site. A total of 4.5 inches of rain fell in the Nassau area. The flooding affected the site and impacted the downstream waterways, residences, and well water.

Clean-up of unwanted chemicals like PCBs and microplastics in the environment is made that much more difficult by extreme weather events.

And more frequent extreme weather events are at least in part caused by increased levels of CO2 in the atmosphere, which in turn is the result of unchecked consumption.

The three are linked. The spread of PCBs and microplastics is aided and exacerbated by ravenous consumption.

Were there more compelling reasons to get into a sustainability boat than I had already found? If there were, I could not see them and what I was learning made the struggle to identify them seem incapable of producing any result.

The first 20 years of my life, I grew up near a polluted lake but ignored the problem. The next 30 years, I worked in my family's plastic bag manufacturing firm and ignored the end-of-life issue. For all 50 years of my life, I have been a free-wheeling consumer. Consuming, using, and disposing without much regard to the circularity of products, of chemicals, of carbon release, or of those affected by this linear way of life.

Polluted lake, plastic bags, unconstrained consumerism. Three strikes.

When I began my journey, I had wanted to try to better understand the lake and distance myself from the cause. The reverse had happened. I now seemed to have more in common with the cause and have further distanced myself from the lake.

Maybe I embodied the problem. I did not dump PCBs into a landfill, but I had been dumping carbon into the environment and plastics into the marketplace all while ignoring the end-of-life issues those actions create.

PCBs, microplastics, and consumerism have in many ways defined my journey. All invisible, all easy to overlook, and all wielding potential catastrophic effects.

The powerlessness and sadness I experienced watching the smoke rise from Delson's embers returned 38 years later just two miles up the road as I stared at the lake.

The momentum to find out more was fading and with little motivation to continue to self-educate, I had little other reason to keep going. My way of understanding suddenly felt hopelessly incomplete. My research, interviews, and the idea that I could find answers—and a way forward—suddenly seemed futile and foolish.

I stopped writing.

I stopped going to the lake.

Chapter 12

AND THE GREATEST IS...

was stuck. Suddenly, I didn't have a purpose to what I was trying to do and why I was trying to do it. I was engulfed by a tidal wave of doubt. As I fought to find a way back to my path of investigation, I reflected on all my experiences in the outdoors. And it worked. Following those memories reminded me of why I had begun this environmentalist journey.

My family went cross-country skiing at Mount Van Hoevenberg in Lake Placid, New York—the host of the 1980 Olympics Nordic ski events. We were excited to be skiing the same trails Olympians had years before. Spread over 1,000 acres, 50 kilometers of trails wound through the dark forest, a dizzying maze surrounding the lodge. The maze turned out to be a problem.

I waited downslope for my sons to appear, but even as I squinted, I couldn't see them. Had they decided to venture off? How could they have? There was only one path leading to me, or so I thought.

I waited. Each minute felt longer than the one before. I had seen them just a few minutes ago—they'd been right behind me.

Where were they?

The thousands of pine trees surrounding the trail were smothered with snow from the prior night's storm. They appeared like sherpas hoping to unload their cargo. The forest, which until then had been a source of beauty and liberation suddenly revealed its vast expanse and danger. My two boys might be wandering lost in this sea of dense wood.

My layers of clothes grew stifling and uncomfortable, and my brain ached. What to do? Think.

Tick….tick….tick. Seven or eight minutes had passed. Far too long. Something must have happened.

Waiting was no longer acceptable. I had two options. Remove my skis and walk back up the slope a quarter mile or ski the rest of the slope and pick up the start of the trail to circle back to the place I'd last seen them—about half a mile in full. Skiing would likely be faster. That's what I did.

After one last hopeful look back up the hill revealed nothing, I took off the other way to get to the trailhead. Adrenaline filled my veins fueled by fear, my irresponsibility, and determination. I raced along, doing my best impression of an Olympian in pursuit of the medal stand. The trail, the trees, and the snow blended into one making me think I was almost there at every turn.

Tick…tick…tick. With sunset just an hour away, fear of the worst kind was beginning to dominate my thoughts. What if… No. I could not go there.

Sweat poured out of my ski hat and into my eyes. The salt stung but there was no time to stop. Legs burning, arms weakening, and back aching, my appreciation for the professionals who do this for hours on end grabbed a sliver of my mind. I turned the corner to where I was sure was the last place I'd seen them.

And there they were.

"Oh... Hi Dad!" both my sons said in unison as if I'd just got home from work. I saw a few snow angels off to the side.

"What have you been doing?" I asked.

"Christian's ski fell off and we couldn't get it back on. We figured you would be back in a few minutes," Ben said.

To them, with less sense of time, the 20 minutes we'd been separated felt like only two. For me, it was the reverse—every two felt like 20. I realized they weren't remotely affected by the event like I was. Lesson learned.

Energized by finding my sons, we secured the skis and were soon gliding along on the trail. We raced back to the lodge with the promise of meeting up with my wife and four-year-old hanging closer to the lodge for hot chocolate and snacks. The lure of food and the assignment that those two were Team USA and I, the Russian, in hot pursuit created a race to the finish for our memories. This assured that they would stay in front of me.

We skied for 20 minutes straight. They kept looking back to see if I was gaining on them. We broke through the forest at the end of the trail to the open space. It was a sprint to the finish, and they pushed themselves all the way to the lodge to hold me off. We were all Olympians that day.

When we arrived, my wife and youngest son were waiting. The number of people still around was dropping as fast as the temperature. Before we all began to take off our hats, gloves, and boots, we just sat for a moment on an empty bench outside the lodge.

The kids were visibly tired, all looking with blank stares and red cheeks into the wilderness across the open snow-covered clearing. The high bright sun that once glistened the snow was now creating conical shadows as it set behind northern pines lining the perimeter. My wife had closed her eyes, her chin turned up to capture as much late afternoon sun as possible.

I looked at my family—the four of them in a row. The smell of crisp mountain air, feel of the cold, white ground, brilliance of the still high blue sky, sight of sunbeams fighting to get through branches, and the enormity of the forest and love for my family and surroundings filled my heart. I was happy and so were they.

The memory of that day helped to reset me on my journey.

I found a renewed desire to help the outdoors that has served me over a lifetime. The other thing that I had always leaned on in times of indecision and reflection was my faith. Maybe the two were linked.

Nassau Reformed Church was the church I attended as a kid. It sat a quarter of a mile east of the main traffic light in the village. Less than half a mile from my house, we would sometimes walk home after the service through the village.

The sidewalk, a walkway to the entrance, and just a 10-yard-wide strip of lawn separated the church from the main road. Multiple roof peaks, wall-sized ornate stained-glass windows, and the sheer size of the building caused some rubber-necking as cars passed by.

The walkway led up seven or eight steep stairs to large, dark wood-stained double doors that opened to a vestibule. Once inside, the rounded room was 15–20 feet in diameter. Two thick ropes hung on the outside circumference behind the door when it was opened. The ropes seemed to be cut from the same production run as those that moor large boats in an angry sea—they extended the 20-foot height of the room and disappeared into the wood ceiling above. Just before church began the ropes were yanked to rock the large bell above, which issued an announcement of the imminent start of the service. The front area also served as the home for the baptismal font and as the point of entry to the main church to the right and to the back rooms of the building to the left.

The back of the building housed a large gathering area, four religious education classrooms, and a bathroom. Mrs. McKever and Mrs. LeFevre were tasked with teaching children about faith. They did it with patience, soothing voices, and a message of hope and love that young minds could grasp. They did it in those rooms for many, many years.

I was one of those children. I will be forever grateful to them and countless others who formed my faith at a young age. The seeds they planted and watered would not be fully grown for decades. If I could, I would tell them their time and efforts have helped me navigate life the best way I can. Funny, but something tells me they already knew this.

To the right in the vestibule, a double glass entry door led to the main church. The grandeur of the interior did not seem to fit its small-town setting.

The sanctuary was a wide pie shape with a stage and pulpit at the smaller end. Entry from the vestibule was at the upper left side of the crust when facing the stage. The walkway in the back was flanked on the right by the enormous stained-glass windows visible from the road and to the left rows of pews angled toward the stage with each row slightly lower and narrower than the one before it. Standing center crust with the window behind, an 8-foot cross hanging above and behind the stage was on an even sight line. Elevation declined with every step walking down the main aisle toward the stage. Ten to fifteen rows of pews extended to the right and left to welcome up to 300 or 400 people. To the right of the stage was the organ, two rows of benches for the chorus, and another wall-sized stained-glass window. The cavernous space was capped by an angled ceiling full of interlocking wood beams embedded at various angles creating a wide array of triangular shapes.

I always thought the shape of the worship space enhanced the service. Reverend Lazaro was a short, portly man, a gifted orator with a booming voice and the warmest heart. His position at the pulpit was at the lowest point of the sanctuary. While he was the messenger, he never came across as any better than any of us and his location on the same plane or lower spoke to that idea. We were all in this together—all trying to learn and to follow what our faith teaches without judgment.

I found myself on that stage a few times. With just a few kids per grade in faith formation, the role of Joseph at Christmas Eve services often fell to me as we re-enacted the nativity scene. With curtain up at 7:00 p.m., we would arrive an hour in advance to get dressed into our costumes.

The first layer was a loose-fitting, off white, long-sleeve cotton shirt with some fancy stitching near the neckline and some tighter threads around the wrist. The outer tunic was a square with a hole for the head. The poncho was a patchwork of faded browns, tans, reds, and blues with the arms cut back. My transformation into Joseph was complete with a dirt brown wide band of cloth that served as a belt. It helped prevent the oversized robe from completely limiting movement. After tying the cloth around my waist, the ends would hang just below my knees.

Joseph had no speaking lines, but still, my nerves grew as showtime approached. The church lights would dim and only a few spotlights remained, shining on the main stage. We would enter from the vestibule and walk the length of the main aisle to our places on stage where Mrs. Lefevre would be crouched, guiding us with positioning and what to say. After our performance, the congregation would stand and sing *Away in a Manger*. Being on stage in costume, a congregation standing with keen interest, low lights in the voluminous space, and voices celebrating in song captured a feeling I will always recall.

For that moment, I was Joseph.

But who was Joseph? The husband of Mary and human father to Jesus is the quick answer. While his presence in the Bible is limited, his faith, willingness to listen, to obey and to sacrifice were not.

Joseph chose to believe the voices of angels that the child Mary carried was the Son of God. He poured himself into his wife and Son. He gave up his carpentry means of living to move his wife and child out of harm's way. He risked whatever social status was in place for a man marrying a pregnant woman. He married Mary knowing the laws at the time for unwed pregnant women was potential stoning.

He was selfless, quiet, sacrificial, and regarded others as more important than himself.

In 2021 I went back to the place I had stood on stage 40 years earlier. That place is now a patch of grass—the church was condemned due to structural issues. Without the funds to fortify it, there was no choice but to tear down the historical icon. The building is gone.

Gone too are Reverend Lazzaro, Mrs. McKever, and Mrs. LeFevre. Mrs. McKever passed away in March 2021. I received a social media post of her passing as I wrote this chapter. Her obituary made no mention of her Sunday School teachings. She donated her time and her talents without the need for recognition. So did the others, just like Joseph. Their influences and stories live on in all they touched. They represent the best expression of community, faith, and love that I can think of.

"Thou shalt love the Lord thy God with all thy heart, and with all thy soul, and with all thy mind. This is the first and greatest commandment. And the second is like unto it, thou shalt love thy neighbor as thyself."[97]

Loving thy neighbor. What does that mean exactly? I think love refers to unconditional commitment and neighbor means all things in the environment. If I depend on and affect the environment and all things depend on and affect the environment, then I depend on and affect all things through how I treat the environment.

Loving the environment seems to me to be a real act of loving thy neighbor.

Toxic chemicals on land and in waterways, global warming, and air pollution all negatively impact the environment and in turn directly affect us. We do not love our neighbor when we damage the environment.

Faith and science help us see what we otherwise cannot. We can't see the future, so we need tools to help us create a better one.

Science to help guide and faith to provide moral motivation. Love is the tour guide for these two. Love of humanity and all living things. Love of those who will come after us.

My memory of our family in Lake Placid drives me to be better. To not try to live more sustainably would mean that my kids will have less chance of recreating that experience with their future families and beyond. That memory keeps me moving as it will for future generations if we give them the chance to live it for themselves.

Maybe the most powerful reason to get into the boat is love. I think we all love the Earth and I think we all love our families and friends and cling to the idea of providing for the future of life.

My exhaustion from finding more questions than answers, frustrations of being just a small link in a massive chain of change, self-doubt, guilt, and apathy, and from a lifetime of blind immersion in the pit of environmental issues is buoyed back up and strengthened by the image of my family in the Lake Placid woods.

Back on the trail that winter day, I was temporarily paralyzed by inaction. I waited to see my young kids' ski hats crest the hill. But they didn't. At some point, waiting was no longer an option.

I can wait for the answer to show itself or I can resolve to find answers myself, move past the poor decisions that led me to this place and move with determination and urgency. Thankfully, I decided to move that day, which resulted in a framed picture for a lifetime. I do not have a photograph of my young sons and my wife on the bench outside the lodge absorbing the last rays of the cold January sun that day. I do not need one. That image is a permanent part of me.

The image is a motivational reminder of nature, family,

preservation, faith, and time. I want more of these images to reflect on. I want more people to have similar images.

Love is a major motivator. It has helped me realize what is most important to overcome the obstacles of guilt, inadequacy, ignorance, and laziness.

I was uplifted by reflecting on my past with clear thoughts on the motivating factors of love of family, friends, neighbors, and nature. I needed to find ways to uplift others.

I was ready to go back to the lake to listen once again.

Chapter 13

NUDGES

When I began my journey, the lake was just something on the side of the road—a one-dimensional backdrop as I raced by, year after year.

An experience in Yosemite National Park changed all that.

Standing atop Vernal Falls in Yosemite National Park offered a vision of a wild trip down the gorge. The water from heights well beyond our vision powers passed us to get to the edge of the cliff before falling to the pool below. The 317-foot fall culminates in a deafening crash before the water re-orients to continue its more leisurely descent down the valley with steep rocky walls guarding the sides. The repetitiveness of the water flow has a hypnotic effect. Water gushing, splashing, and crashing in its approach. Water falling, calming, and silencing as it moves down the narrow canyon. Over and over.

"Dad...Dad," our nine-year-old was calling.

My trance was broken by the kids' readiness to leave. We had a choice. Walk back down the steep and narrow trail that hugged the water or take a more circuitous route. The stream of people coming up the trail rendered the people going back down the salmon swimming upstream. We chose the longer, less crowded route. We sold it to our kids as the road less traveled although that analogy likely fell on deaf ears. The kids led the charge, my wife and I following behind with the map.

"Do we even know where we are going?" the tribe asked and asked again as time wore on.

Trail markers were few and far between. The lure of the pool back at the lodge was strong in our kids' minds. They began to think it was less the trail markers and more the trail reader causing the seeming aimless direction we were headed. They were likely correct—we were still hiking up the gorge to find the trail back down.

Eventually, we spotted some people, the first we'd seen in 30 minutes. Their trail hats, water bottles, backpacks, maps sticking out of multiple pockets, and hiking shoes qualified them as a trustworthy source of directions. Their guidance proved worthy. Finally, we found the John Muir Trail.

The 220-mile John Muir trail extends through much of the Sierra Nevada Mountain range. Its namesake, John Muir, was a preservationist, naturalist, founder of the Sierra Club, father of America's national parks, guardian angel of American wilderness, and so much more. His ideas, essays, and actions in the 1800s and early 1900s set a foundation for today's environmentalism. He welcomed then President Roosevelt in 1903 for what we discovered back in Chapter 3 as a path-dependent trip, forming the last 120 years history of environmental protection.

While the trail we had walked up was direct and steep, the

trail back was a long, more gradual descent. It switch-backed for almost an hour but knowing we were now on the right path had injected some life into the boys. My wife and I hung back, watching them chatter happily.

With the complaint department closed, we were able to enjoy the walk. The smell of pine, sun darting through the canopy above, and ancient steel-gray rock visible in all directions fulfilled what we had seen in the brochure. Hiking in Yosemite was exactly as advertised.

During our week-long visit to Yosemite Valley, we made it to many of the tourist attractions. Glacier Point offered sweeping, unencumbered views of the valley below, standing at the base of El Capitan provided a sense of place, and Yosemite Falls gave us a family picture we will always cherish. Oddly, as I reflect on our trip, it was not those events that struck my core. It was the descent down John Muir Trail.

It was entirely possible that we walked in the same footsteps that John Muir had. Being there with the surroundings likely looking very similar touched off something in me as time separated us from the trip. I look back and think that at least internally, that hike passed an invisible tiny environmental torch. A torch that forced me to ask that internal question I had suppressed for far too long.

"When was I going to act?"

A question I hadn't yet answered. Even now I haven't fully answered it.

However, that hike gave me a nudge and a light to start.

AGENT-BASED MODELING

I think the environment is something most people love, cherish, think about, and know we need to preserve. I don't think people *want* to exacerbate global warming, reduce biodiversity, or hamstring future generations' ability to inhabit the planet. What people differ over is the degree and urgency to which sustainability warrants the need to change. As individuals, how do we summon the energy to galvanize what we are feeling out into the world in the form of real action? What will make us climb into our sustainability boat?

Agent-Based Modeling or ABM offers some help. Broadly defined, ABM gives agents (variables) initial behavior rules that organize their actions and interactions. The model of these interaction rules is repeated numerous times to obtain a distribution of possible outcomes. The number of agents, complexity of the interactions, adaptations of agents, and length of time can all be changed to accommodate the situation and to provide the most accurate model. A simple example helped me better understand this modeling tool.[98]

Modeling greedy cows versus cooperative cows. Cows are the agents—the things that act in the model as time elapses. Cows interact with the environment by feeding on a patch of grass. They feed for a set amount of time and then wander over to another patch. Two opposite behavior rules for the cows' eating habits were assigned. Some are assigned as "greedy" cows where they eat all their patch of grass and save nothing. A red square represents a greedy cow. The other cows are assigned as "cooperative" where they save some grass on their patch for the next visitor. A green square represents a cooperative cow. The cows reproduce by color if they have had enough to eat.

At the beginning, the "field of grass" on the computer screen is filled with red or green squares representing the grass inhabited by cows. In running the model, the cows move from patch to patch after a set amount of time elapses. As they move, we see the green and red squares, which are equal in number at the start, change and move towards a red dominated landscape. All things being equal, the red greedy cows are not playing by the same rules as the green cooperative cows and thus eat more and reproduce more. With less to eat and because they're trying to save some grass for the next cow, the green cows die faster. Red cows begin to dominate but—and here's the crux—they too eventually die off as there are no green cows and thus no conservation of grass to eat for the next inhabiting cow.

Red cows—all about pure survival with no regard to the common good—thrive in the short term but die off in the longer term. Not recognizing the need to preserve for the future means, both red and green cows will eventually die out. The greedy cows' mentality is not sustainable.

When the model is changed to include some social behavior where the green cows protect their own and influence surrounding patches of grass to save, a different color field is revealed. This change creates a more balanced result over time—both red and green cows survive and there is enough food for all.

The model shows that not every cow needs to be green. If there are enough green cows and they act in a protective way, there is enough to eat for all. The proactive green cows "cover" for the greedy red ones.

Some people who do little for the environment (red cows) can't be green or can't be as green as they would like to be because of finances, know-how, or circumstance. Some red cows don't want to be green because they don't perceive the need to change as urgent or even real. They pursue their own good at the potential expense of societal long-term needs. Green cows, then, who pursue their own good while also serving the common good, need to make up for these red cows.

Waiting for others to act results in inaction and a suffering environment.

Cow modeling is very simple. The model increases exponentially in complexity when factors like other animals, weather, location, etc. are introduced, but even the simple model brings to light the core question:

How can we incentivize the common good and become green, or at least a shade of green (or less red)? Conversely, how do we de-incentivize pure self-serving behavior?

Government mandates can incentivize green cow behavior. An example of government action to enhance sustainability is California Senate Bill 1383, effective January 1, 2022. The bill sets a target to reduce the disposal of organic waste in landfills, including edible food. The goal is to reduce statewide organic waste by 75% by 2025. The bill addresses three key statistics:

- 40% of food is wasted

- Approximately 1 in 4 Californians are struggling with food insecurity

- Food waste accounts for 8% of global emissions mainly through methane and CO2 emitted from landfills

The bill mandates food service businesses must donate edible surplus food to food recovery organizations; organics are to be separated, collected, and turned into compost; and composters must be made available to each person in each municipality.

The policy is designed to feed the hungry, enable the composting industry to grow, prevent greenhouse gas emissions, and divert organics away from landfills.

Energy costs help us act like green cows. Since 2009, investment in new generating capacity for energy has doubled for renewables and has been cut by 50% for fossil fuels. The result of past and present investment has energy approaching "grid parity"—the point where the cost of using renewables is at or below the cost of using fossil fuels. As the cost drops, the change to renewables accelerates.[99]

Social influence helps us act like green cows. What our neighbors do influences us and vice versa. The green cows turned the tide when they influenced the red cows.

When we act like green cows, paths emerge along commonly traveled routes. People tend to travel routes that others have taken, making them more attractive to future travelers.

These paths can also appear as "nudges." Nudges change the way people look at choices in a way that makes them more likely to pick the opinion that benefits them the most. Intentions are always ahead of behaviors. We have good intentions on many things like weight loss, health, and saving more but tangible supporting actions often trail well behind those intentions. "Nudges" help us to get traction.

A grocery store offers an example of a nudge to buy healthy food. The store created a glossy placard that hangs inside food carts. The placard mimics a mirror. The store also displayed signs telling shoppers how much produce the average customer was buying. Both the mirror and displays were nudges to get shoppers to change their shopping habits in a healthier direction.[100]

What are the social influences and nudges we can use to create routes to sustainability?

Solar panels, rain collection barrels, community advocacy groups, electric cars, wind turbines, recycle bins, composters, reusable grocery bags, bike paths, and community clean-up efforts are all visible nudges.

Many behaviors are invisible to the public but highly visible to the common good. Behaviors like taking shorter showers, using LED lights in the home, charitable giving to environmental causes, investing in companies who engage in sustainable practices, and sponsoring vulnerable children or families, domestic or overseas.

With 72% of global emissions traced back to the home, the decisions we make every day have a huge impact.[101]

Installing electric heat pumps instead of using gas or oil in homes moves away from fossil fuel dependence and reduces CO2 emissions.[102] Buying clothes made from recycled cotton and polyester fibers pulls materials from waste streams thereby reducing the demand for virgin materials. Eating a more plant-based diet and consuming less meat and dairy helps reduce emissions, which accounts for 14.5% of global greenhouse gas emissions according to the UN Food and Agriculture Organization.[103]

Changing how we heat our homes, how we buy our clothes, and how we eat, are all personal nudges toward sustainability. A lot of small behaviors can add up to big changes for good. And once the cumulative effect is visible, widespread behavior change is more likely.

Over the course of many visits on foot, on my bike, and in the kayak, the lake has nudged me. What I thought of as the lake's secrets were the exact opposite. The lake is alive, has a voice, and has always been communicating. There never were any secrets. I finally saw that a cocktail of the busyness and the business of life, ignorance, apathy, and lack of compassion had blurred my vision and weakened my judgment.

The more time I spent there, the more the lake had given me nudges and taught me lessons to carry forward. I began to hear what my friend was saying, prompting clearer thinking, positive rhetoric, and action. Ten takeaways emerged.

1. Stop dumping waste. Dumping is what caused the issue in the first place. The physical dumping of toxic chemicals in the landfill in turn polluted the lake for generations. For residents of Nassau living around the waste dump, PCBs along with other found chemicals like 1,4-dioxane still remain today. The known carcinogens sit in the current dump site, the underwater aquifers, the streams that run away from the site, the Valatie Kill, and Nassau Lake itself. The health concerns, land devaluation, and mental anguish is all still there. While open pit toxic dumping has been curtailed by a multitude of regulatory laws and governing bodies, dumping of a different sort is now most pressing.

My grandparents were my age when the toxic dumping started in 1952. Their grandparents were my age when one of the most influential papers on the link between levels of CO_2 and the Earth's temperature was published. The 1896 paper by Noble Prize-winning Swedish chemist Svante Arrhenius was the first to put hard data to the greenhouse gas effect.[104] We have known about the perils of dumping CO_2 into the atmosphere for over 100 years.

My kids are the fifth generation from the late 1800s. Each

generation that has passed the CO2 baton to the next has done so making the next leg of the run more strenuous. At some point, the run will turn to a walk, a crawl, and, if the path becomes too steep, full surrender.

2. Circularity is a first-order principle. If circular principles had been fully understood and in place in the early 1900s, manufacturing processes would not produce toxic chemicals. In a circular economy, there is no waste. A by-product for one process is feedstock for another. This is achieved by looking at the whole process and designing with the end in mind.

Circularity also recognizes that the Earth's resources are limited. We need to reduce what we use, and reuse materials that already exist. We need to consume less. Unlimited growth through increased consumption in a limited resource world is not sustainable. Consuming less translates to fewer materials, fewer emissions, and less energy wastage. How do we do this and keep economies afloat with the world population growing?

One way is to move toward a service-based economy. Circularity is more about use of goods and not possessing goods. Today, the incentive for a producer is to make a product last long enough that you are satisfied but for a short enough time that you will soon need to buy a new one. Producers do not have an overwhelming incentive to make long-lasting products as that will cost future sales.

A service-based economy incentivizes the producers to make the best product item they can and service the item throughout its life. The consumer pays for the item at a discount (or not at all) and enters a contract to pay a monthly fee for the use of the item. The lease program puts the responsibility back on the manufacturer to make the best, most durable item they can, so they limit the expense of servicing the product.

A good example is leasing a high-quality washing machine that lasts 15 to 20 years and is remanufactured and repaired throughout its usable life. Fewer machines, fewer materials. Two or three cheaper machines could be replaced by one longer lasting one. The producer wants to make the highest quality machine it can, both to avoid repairs and to have the best machine possible for refurbishment at the end of life.

Total annual municipal solid waste generation in the United States has increased by 93% since 1980 to 292 million tons per year.[105] An American weighing 180 lbs generates their own weight in waste every 37 days.

The goal should be to buy less and highly value what we have. Not the other way around. A capitalist service-based economy and the promotion of high-quality goods helps to transition away from an economy based on high consumption of lower quality goods.

The key word is transition. With more infrastructure already in place to make goods rather than service them, it will take time to change. The washing machine company that invested in factories to make high volumes of washing machines likely did not also invest in a large number of technicians to service them. It will take time to reverse the model to factories building fewer machines while building an army of technicians to keep those machines in use. The revenue generated by the company still grows but the dollars come from paying for the service to use the machines and not for the machines themselves.

The underlying principle for an economy that does not rely on consuming goods at an endless pace is circularity.

3. Mother Nature. As my visits to the lake became more frequent and I spent more time alone there, I thought about the term Mother Nature. In particular, the word Mother. Mothers give and nurture. They have a soft side for their children that never wanes. If we think of nature as a Mother, as a living being, our psychology around how we treat nature changes. When we borrow from someone, we give back. When we need something from someone, we ask if it's possible to do it without harm. When we see someone in need, we help.

A psychological shift toward compassion and humanizing nature is needed to put the 'Mother' back into Mother Nature.

4. Voices. The lake had a voice. It spoke through the many people I met along my journey. Two people's voices in particular echo in my head when I think about, visit, and drive past the lake, even to this day.

David and Rita Labrum have lived on the northern end of Nassau Lake for 49 years. The front of their property has a view of the lake from the eastern side. The primary road I have traveled so many times corralling the water on the western side was directly across the water, a half mile away. To the right of their property is the inlet of water where the Valatie Kill flows into the lake—the primary conduit the chemicals take from the landfill.

I visited the Labrums on a sunny summer afternoon. Rita and David talked about the history of their house, some family memories, and their work prior to retirement. After exchanging some old stories about Nassau we both shared in the 1970s and 1980s, the conversation shifted to the pollution.

"When you bought the house in the early 1970s, did you know what had happened in the landfill decades prior?" I asked.

"No," said Rita. "I don't think anyone really knew anything

for at least a few more years."

Rita told me she served as the town clerk for decades.

"Was Dewey Loeffel Landfill ever asked to talk to the town about the pollution?"

"There were lots of hearings over the years, but I don't recall ever having a dump site representative present. Engineers from ENCON (New York State Department of Environmental Conservation), promising this and that seemed to be the ones there. Not much seemed to get accomplished," she replied.

We chatted for 45 minutes. They didn't hold bitterness over what had happened and what had not happened to address the issue. But they did hold hope for a resolution.

Rita's eyes lit up when I mentioned some Superfund sites had been cleaned up and were on a path to recovery.

"Really? That is my hope." Both felt it may not happen in their lifetime but remain optimistic.

I asked them if they liked living there, even knowing what they knew. This was the question I was most curious about. If I was to find the lake's voice, then listening to the people who worked hard, served the community, bought a home on its shores decades before, and never left was the best way of capturing it.

Mr. Labrum paused and looked to the west from his recliner. The view through the storm door and bank of windows revealed an unencumbered view of the lake. Sunlight glistened off the water straight into the house. A distant green background of a low hill framed a view that never changes.

"The sun sets right over there. It's beautiful. It's quiet and seeing the wildlife year-round is nice too," he said.

There was another pause after he spoke. While I did not know the Labrums, the pause was the opposite of awkward. The pause was their invite to me to share the view they had both enjoyed for 49 years. I was grateful.

"This is our home," Rita said.

Mine too, I thought.

5. Learn. Onondaga Lake sits in the heart of Syracuse, New York. It is 1 mile wide and 4½ miles long. Once referred to as the most polluted lake in America, it was crushed by both raw and partially treated sewage from the surrounding areas and decades of industrial dumping.

A party responsible for much of the industrial pollution was Solvay Process Company, which became Allied Signal, who merged with Honeywell International.[106] The lake was put on the federal National Priority List for Superfund sites in 1994. Since then, Honeywell International with oversight from the EPA, NYSDEC, and the NYS Department of Health has performed clean-up work to re-vitalize the lake.

Over 2 million cubic yards of material were removed from Onondaga Lake. About 2.5 billion gallons of water were treated. Approximately 475 acres of the lake have been capped to offer a new habitat layer and isolate remaining contamination. Over 1 million native plants, trees, and shrubs are being planted and about 90 acres of wetlands have been created or enhanced.[107] After 30 years and more than a $1 billion clean-up, the lake is making a comeback.[108]

The Onondaga Lake story offers hope that recovery is possible. I visited the Honeywell Onondaga Lake Visitor Center on an August afternoon.

The building provides educational experiences surrounding what happened to the lake and what has and is being done to address the issue. Engaging displays and enlarged photographs provide colorful visuals of the bird, fish, animal, and plant life in the area and tell the lake's story. The building is also a meeting space for public gatherings.

I spent 45 minutes there and realized the building is much more than the physical structure. It seemed to be a symbol of trust to the public. Providing information, charting progress, and holding public meetings builds trust. Trust that the contamination was being removed, treated, or capped to return the lake to its original state—a return of boating, fishing, swimming, and wildlife.

The activity in and around the lake was evidence that the project was showing signs of success. The parking lot surrounding the visitor center was filling up with vehicles pulling boats to get into the water at the adjacent boat launch. A wide view of the lake saw multiple boats zipping along.

The more I learned on this journey, the more hope I began to stockpile. It became a comfort knowing others have traveled this same path, knew the frustrations of inaction, and saw a better future. My heart swelled as I drove home with renewed hope that things can change.

The Onondaga Lake Visitor Center is a museum of sorts. It's a place that helps us all remember, raises awareness, and continues to allow us to learn from the past.

A Nassau Lake Visitor Center someday could provide the same benefit. We want to be aware of what happened, have reverence for those affected, and understand why it happened all while trying to prevent it from happening again.

6. Resilience. The waters of Nassau Lake will outlive all of us. The PCBs in the lake will one day dissipate. There is hope in this. However, the time from PCB breakdown varies widely based on the chemical composition, and conditions surrounding the chemicals—shallow water, deep water, exposure to sunlight, temperature, microorganisms present in the lake bed, etc.

The rate of breakdown in water sediment "is slow and even the lower chlorinated compounds present some risk, so EPA determined that natural breakdown was not by itself sufficient to address concerns posed by PCB's."[109]

If left to cure itself, it will likely take the lake 200-plus years to rid itself of PCBs.

In three separate trips to the lake, I gazed at bald eagles soaring above and was able to find one nesting at the very top of a tree on the water's edge. In repeated sightings, the majestic birds came to represent nature finding its way through the pollution to re-establish itself.

The Earth is about 4.6 billion years old and will continue to adapt. The lake has already and will continue to adjust. I wonder if we will be able to.

I started out feeling sorry for the lake. I now think it is the reverse.

7. Idleness. For as long as I can remember, I have always been doing something. Checking off things on the to-do list, then adding more, creating a treadmill of tasks that will last a lifetime. I have always viewed doing nothing as sitting somewhere between being lazy, unmotivated, and lacking ambition. Always being busy tricked my mind into thinking that doing something equated with *accomplishing* something. Doing something trumped doing nothing. The lake has brought me behind the stage to see the secrets of the trick.

I have been busy for 50 years. I have driven by the lake thousands of times, always too immersed in my to-do list to stop. Visiting the lake over and over in my quest to find answers, I did very little other than think. I was idle on the lake, idle sitting on shore, idle in my car, idle on my bike. Thinking. Relaxing. It helped me gain a perspective I never had before.

During these times, the lake seemed idle. With little to no activity on it, the water is often very calm. The surface acts like a mirror to the surrounding landscape and the beauty of the surrounding trees and shore-side homes is framed within it.

In my own idleness, I found that doing nothing *is* actually doing something, and doing something may in fact not achieve anything at all. Doing nothing leads to thought, which in turn leads to action. Something happens but only in time. The magician flashes "something" as a diversion—a constant distraction so the audience never sees the magic of nothingness.

8. Don't be a red cow. I think the lake would ideally like us to all be green cows but seems satisfied to simply ask that we are not all red. Even just a little green is okay. Too many red cows not trying to influence the common good will lead to disaster. A shade of green, however, recognizes the planet as a stakeholder and the need to preserve it for long-term survival.

9. Precautionary Principle. Taking time to think has been an unforeseen and crucial part of this journey. I was always too busy to think. I just wanted to get the job done. In school, I studied to get good grades, not to learn. I think I have adopted that mindset too much in life: get things done, check off my list, move on. Thinking, on the other hand, pumps the brakes on the wheels of the brain—it slows us right down.

Thinking helped me understand that the simple explanation was not always the right explanation. Knowing what I do not want was just as important as knowing what I do want.

The precautionary principle is a broad thinking approach that is characterized by slowing down, exploring a wide range of alternatives, increasing the number of people in the decision-making process, gathering more complete information and considering second- and third-hand effects before making decisions. The approach helps to minimize risk and future damage especially if the potential impacts are irreversible, hard to contain, or impact people who didn't choose to be involved.

The people of Nassau did not choose to be involved.

10. Reflection. In the middle of Nassau Lake one bright sunny weekend afternoon, with no one there but me, I look straight down off the side of my boat. I had done this before—I wanted to see the PCBs. See what had caused the generational angst. Gain clarity of the enemy. Each time, I failed to find the culprit to quench my thirst. On this last trip of the year the depths below fade into the background as my eyes refocus on the surface.

The glimmer of sun reflects off the water. Slight ripples pass under my boat, rocking it gently. My eyes lock onto the surface. I see something. I touch the water to break the surface and blur the image. The water quickly re-settles and I see it again.

It's me.

It's my reflection on the surface. It always has been. It was there when I was skipping rocks from the shore as a boy at the then local eatery, as a teen as I stared out the bus window, and as an adult as I drive the parallel road.

The lake has always been there. Patient. Steady. Vigilant. Waiting for me to see my own reflection.

I saw it. The lake's ultimate secret is not a secret at all. If we can see nature as a reflection of ourselves, the path to take becomes self-evident. I was not there to help the lake. The lake was there to help me. The lake helped me engage in a candid dialogue with myself.

Seeing my reflection that day helped me start to sort through my past and address the obstacles I had always been struggling over.

I realized that any change to future actions would only come from confronting the gang of bandits I'd uncovered during my journey. These are the characters who lurk in the shadows preventing us from getting into our sustainability boats.

It was time to take them down.

Chapter 14

SHOWDOWN

My hope had been to find reasons for people to get into their sustainability boats. And I thought I'd managed to do that. The task had seemed straightforward but had grown in complexity as the reasons I was finding were simultaneously uncovering hidden reasons to resist. The lake had helped reveal the bandits who steal motivation, replace will with apathy, and co-join survival and preservation with an *or* not an *and*.

The lake inspired me to round up the thieves I had identified and bring them to the shore for questioning. The lake had let me struggle on this journey—questioned my past, challenged my audacity to address the issues, and undermined my grit to keep going. The lake knew that if I was able to continue, I would identify the primary reasons why it was in its present state. I would go beneath the surface knowledge that toxic chemicals had done this. The bandits stealing circularity and preventing people from finding their sustainability boats would face their victim.

The cast of bandits and I assembled at the water's edge on

the half-mile narrow strip of land on the western side of the lake. The spot offered sweeping views of the water. The rounded green hills in the distance beyond the long eastern shoreline were barely visible as darkness held its grip. We had gathered at 5 o'clock on a late summer morning. Sunrise was 5:20 a.m.

Ownership, selfishness, not in my backyard, not a big deal, we have time, small actions are inconsequential, ignorance, convenience, cost, politics, regulation, short-termism, apathy, pure profit, survival, economic growth, path of least resistance, closed-mindedness and blaming others were all there. The robbers of sustainability I had encountered throughout the journey were now rounded up for their day of reckoning. The restricted width of land bordering the water naturally formed us all in a line. We stood parallel to the water in a police line-up formation.

What we waited for we didn't know. Some grew restless but still we stood, looking, listening, wondering, and fearing. Fearing that actions each had taken in the past would be exposed by the lake, who suddenly had a voice.

Each suspect in the fictitious line-up loses its power when people prioritize getting into their boats. One by one, the lake addressed the guilty.

Ownership Of Land finds its thievery in exploitation of the land for personal gain. Land ownership can be a positive for the environment when care of personal land recognizes that decisions made are connected to the community at large. Native American communities provide an example of how to treat the environment as a shared resource. The Stockbridge–Munsee Native Americans lived in the Nassau area 300 years before I did. Their care for the environment in viewing nature as a common good to conserve and preserve allows me to enjoy and benefit from it as they did.

My job is to do the same for the person standing here 300 years from now.

Public ownership of land helps keep the negative side of ownership hidden. Perhaps the most basic and effective way to keep the environment healthy is to protect more land and water areas in their natural condition—save more land to save ourselves. In 2020, The United Nations Environment Programme revealed that 17% of the Earth's surface is protected or under conservation efforts.[110] A growing number of scientists are recommending nations commit to increasing this to 30% of land and oceans by 2030 and 50% by 2050.[111]

The bandit *Not in My Backyard* finds its strength in pushing responsibility onto others. Focusing on what we don't want is a counteracting force. If given the choice of windmills or a Superfund site, which would you choose to have in your neighborhood? When we ignore the environment and circular principles to govern the economy, we end up with the latter. Waste dumped 60 years ago led to 1,300-plus Superfund sites in some backyards, including my own. Waste today in the form of carbon emissions into the atmosphere is leading to rising temperatures, climate change, biodiversity loss, and social injustice all of which inhabit all our backyards. I think most of us would accept a windmill in our backyard representing a sustainable future over a Superfund site representing a past of neglect, degradation, and suffering.

Not a Big Deal loses power with investment in awareness. The United Nations Intergovernmental Panel on Climate Change periodic reports continue to sound the alarm of the effects of increasing carbon in the atmosphere. Daily news rings the climate concern bell with reports on increasingly extreme weather causing forest fires, droughts, hurricanes, and tornados. Awareness leads to prioritizing the climate and making it a stakeholder in decisions.

The bandit *Ignorance* becomes less threatening as more education on sustainability invades our minds and more importantly our education system. In 1987, the United Nations produced the report that provided one of the first widely accepted definitions of sustainable development. I graduated from college in 1992. There was no such thing as a sustainability major and the coursework I did take at the time made no mention of the word. Back then the idea and understanding of sustainability was embryonic at most.

Today, it is hard to find a college or university without a sustainability-related concentration or at least coursework devoted to it. My hope is that sustainability education infiltrates the primary and secondary curriculum. As future generations grow up with sustainability embedded in their education, the environment has a much better chance of being a central stakeholder in their decisions.

Small Actions Are Inconsequential is a fraud in realizing that any change begins with a single action, a potentially path-dependent action.

Convenience as a robber is lessened when we lean into the idea of using convenience for what we want. Curbside recycling for all waste, greater access to composting, carbon emission product labels, acceptance of remote working, affordable electric vehicles, electric charging stations as prevalent as gas stations, and electric heat pumps as standard heating and cooling for new construction are all examples that offer convenience and lower emissions.

Politics and Regulation can be a force of positive change when smart policies that view the environment as a key stakeholder are the norm. The more environmental awareness and education the populace can gain, the better chance elected politicians will reflect their desires.

Selfishness, Apathy, and We Got Time lose their power when nudges from green cows influence more sustainable behaviors.

An economy based solely on *Profits, Greed, Growth, Short-Term Gains, and Consumerism* is transitioned to long-termism and service-based growth built on circular ideas when governments and companies come together to enact policies like extended producer responsibility laws and standardized sustainability measurements for public and investor use. Laws and measurements keep governments, people, and companies accountable and on track in transitioning toward sustainability.

In seeing yourself as housing the influences of the bandits, *Blaming Others* is eliminated as a reason not to get into the boat.

Cost and *Path of Least Resistance* are a reduced force when all the other things above are in motion. Circular ideas at scale become the path of least resistance and more cost competitive.

Closed-Mindedness is tamed by changing the goal to be directional and not absolute. Moving in the right direction is better than waiting for the perfect answer. Transition to better systems, products, and policies is about moving from one better directional decision to the next.

There's one left. The hardest one. *Survival.*

Pure survival is not an option. It is not a bandit. Survival is an instinct. One that says if I don't do something, I and my family will not survive. The perceived bandit known as survival is actually love. The instinct to survive is intrinsic to the love of life. Those who are not getting into their sustainability boats are not choosing survival over sustainability. No, they are simply choosing life. No one should have to choose between survival and sustainability. This is where the climate issue as a social justice issue is most acute. Those who are not faced with this choice need to help those who are.

The lake did not speak to all of us that morning, it spoke to all the powerful influences *within* us. The sun opened its eyes on the lake and the lake exposed the bandits that reside in our daily actions. The lake did not assign blame, pass judgment, or unleash retribution but did the opposite. The lake solicited help.

The lake helped me realize *we* are the answer.

The environment needs our help.

People being most affected by damage to the environment need our help.

Loving thy neighbor and by extension loving the environment is the most powerful reason for harnessing the power of bandits within us. It also offers the most compelling reason to get into your sustainability boat toward a better future.

I now know I am the best advocate for the environment but also its greatest threat. This realization may allow me to become something I never considered.

UNLIKELY ENVIRONMENTALIST

There were two questions this book journeyed to answer. All efforts thus far have been focused on the first—to provide reasons to get into your sustainability boat. It is time to address the second—what to do once you're in the boat.

A trip to northern Maine helped me get closer to an answer. A concept called biomimicry—using nature as a guide to learn from.

A few years ago my family and I visited the Jordan Pond House in Acadia National Park. The park was founded in 1916 and sits three-quarters of the way up the coastline of Maine on the northern Atlantic Ocean. The nearly 50,000 acres offers spectacular hiking and biking along wide carriage roads as well as beautiful beaches. It is the only place I have ever been where lush green forest and tall pines butt up against rocky and sandy coastlines.

The long, oval-shaped 27-mile Park Loop Road connects park visitors to trailheads, beaches, vistas, and attractions. At about 7 o'clock on the loop sits Jordan Pond House.

The house traces its roots back to the mid-1800s and by the end of the 19th century, the location had become a popular destination for summer travel. A restaurant emerged from the interest and so began a tradition of popovers and tea overlooking the pond. Tragically, in 1979, a fire destroyed the original building, but the renovated house retains some of the original charm including a stone fireplace, high ceilings, and a lot of exposed wood. Behind the building, a wide lawn extended 200 feet or so to the pond edge. Standing there, I could easily imagine it looked as it might have a century ago. The scenery was peaceful, but the famous popovers were what had first attracted us to make an afternoon reservation.

Thirty plus tables were spread over the lawn with green umbrellas protecting each from the bright sun. In the distance were two round-top, 800-foot mountains known as the North and South Bubbles, which were reflected in the pond's surface. It was a picture postcard of relaxation—or so we thought. As we approached our table, uninvited guests were waiting.

Bees. Not a few, not ten, and not hundreds. Thousands. They were attracted to the sweet food and drink. Their primary targets appeared to be the lemonade and the strawberry jam, but the volume and speed of the bees made anything exposed fair game for attack. Our amazement at their number was outdone only by our incredulity of the wait staff, who seemed to operate without the slightest recognition of their existence.

We decided to give it a go and sit down to see if we could make it through. The server's advice, "Keep still and they will not bother you," was fine in theory, but short-lived in practice. Shooing and waving turned into swatting and flailing at the buzzing dive bombers. When one bee left, it was replaced by two more. It was as if they went back to their hive and told their friends about the open buffet, who in turn told theirs.

Bees communicate through a "waggle" dance to transmit information to members of the hive of a discovered food source. They dance to bring attention, to relate, and to bring better health to the hive. Ultimately, the dance recruits other bees to the targeted food source.

No one was stung and the popovers were as amazing as the setting. Whenever my family reflects on that trip, it's not the food or scenery we recall. It's the bees.

Time for us all to see ourselves as communicators, as educators, as "wagglers"—to bring awareness and provide a clearer sustainability direction. To engage in biomimicry.

What to do once in the boat? Without knowing the next step, people can be reluctant to get in. Heading out on a journey without a destination is like setting the table without having prepared a meal. A walk to a place I had spent the second most time in my life before the age of 13 clarified what I needed to do.

I walked down the sidewalk to the house where my best friend to this day used to live. His parents have lived in the village for 50 years and still do. I wanted to talk to them, to get their perspective on the lake.

I walked up the three steps and knocked on the front door under the protective portico. As the door opened and Mr. Mocerine greeted me, the past overtook the present. The door I had knocked on so many times to ask if my friend could come outside was now an opening to a conversation with cherished neighbors about a lifetime problem.

Mr. Mocerine was a volunteer fireman and my Little League baseball coach. Mrs. Mocerine was involved in the Parent Teacher Organization at the elementary school and worked at the local nursery school around the corner. They were both involved in, cared for, and had contributed to the Nassau community for decades.

Unsurprisingly, our conversation about the lake began with the landfill. On the surface, the landfill owners seemed to be the knee-jerk response to who was responsible for the pollution. Further conversation, however, led to more questions and more responsibility assigned to multiple parties. After the first five minutes, the name Loeffel didn't resurface.

"How much do you think about the lake?" I asked.

"We go about our daily lives as we always have. While we live in the village, the issue seems removed from where we are even though I know it isn't," said Mr. Mocerine.

I asked, "Do you think people outside the area think of Nassau in a different way because of what happened to the lake?"

"I think some people view it as a black eye of sorts."

"Do you think people understand what happened here?" I asked.

"No. Not to the extent we have talked about here."

The last question came from Mrs. Mocerine. She paused, thoughtfully piecing together her words, and asked, "So, what are we supposed to do?" She said it as though it had been on her mind for years, but she didn't know who to ask it to. It seemed a relief to get it out.

I had no real answer at the time, but having embarked on my journey I now know that finding answers and taking action would be the key to real change.

Whether it be Nassau Lake or addressing the climate question at large, four key factors working collectively will provide guidance to moving toward sustainability once people are in their boat.

Awareness. Being aware of what you give your attention to offers a window of choice to choose sustainability. Being aware of sustainability issues, products, concerns, and actions in the community is the first step. Awareness limits the ability to ignore, trumps the business of life as usual, and is a seed to educating ourselves to act.

Like. Apply sustainability awareness and thinking to something you like doing. If you enjoy spending time on the water, join a lake, ocean, or river clean-up effort. If you like wine, learn how climate change can impact viticulture. If taking pictures of nature is your passion, take more and share comments of preservation. If you believe in the business you are in, determine how it can involve itself in environmental, social, and governance (ESG) initiatives. If you like traveling, see if you can offset your emissions by joining organizations that can assist. If you have time to give, join an environmental advocacy group. If you love nature hikes, plant a tree. If you like to learn, read about sustainability issues and solutions.

Build environmentally conscious decisions into your everyday life. Consider giving electric vehicles a test drive. When you cook, make the effort to buy local or grow your own vegetables. When you shop, look for recycled content or the possibility of pre-owned items. When you gather with friends, be an advocate for sustainability when the topic comes up.

Aligning sustainability with your passions provides a map for your boat to follow.

Movement. You are now aware of sustainability efforts in our society. You have a map to pursue sustainability in your passion. Now move. Not act but move. Actions are singular. Movements are not. Movements bring you to a new place where there is more to understand, to learn, and to share. Move.

Signal. To complete the circle, signal to others. When we signal our sustainability journey to others, we nudge them into their own boats. We nudge them to be green cows. The more people in their boats, the more movement.

Awareness. Like. Movement. Signal. ALMS. Almsgiving is the donating of money, time, food, or other items to those in need especially as a spiritual practice. For me, ALMS is a way to consistently remember the direction of the sustainability boat I am in. It is the pulse of sustainability. I am working to learn more, to deepen my passion for the things I love, to move to a different place, to signal to others, and to begin the process again. Once this book is complete, it will signal the need to begin again.

Almsgiving to the environment. That is the direction we must take.

With reasons to get into the boat and direction to travel established, I began to wrestle with the word environmentalist. The word had always struck me as an "extreme" word. Someone labeled or proclaiming to be an environmentalist evoked images of hugging a tree as it was being cut down or camping on a patch of land to prevent a bulldozer from breaking ground on a new development or a speed boat chasing down large fishing vessels flying a flag that said, "Save the Whales."

I now know that an environmentalist is someone concerned with or who advocates for the protection of the environment. A person who is concerned about the destruction or degradation of the Earth through pollution and overuse of finite resources. The images I used to have in my mind are just some examples of how people act out their concern, but I now believe there are countless more ways to demonstrate a love for the planet, all of which fall under an environmentalist umbrella.

From turning off lights to buying recycled content to saving for an electric vehicle, these are all conscious acts to protect the environment. The degree to and speed in which we do them will hasten our movements in a sustainable direction.

But then I discovered a strange statistic. A 2021 Gallup poll found that 41% of Americans identify themselves as environmentalists. The percentage in 1991 was 78%. Why has the percentage dropped so dramatically?[112]

The Gallup poll summation states that part of the decline is tied to greater politicization of environmental issues. While the definition of an environmentalist has not changed, the meaning has. Thirty to 40 years ago, promoting recycling, avoiding the use of harmful chemicals, and reducing serious forms of pollution had gained widespread acceptance. Today, views on global warming, social justice issues, and loss of biodiversity as a result of climate change are more polarized.

The Gallup poll does not define the term "environmentalist" for respondents, rather it let people answer based on their own understanding of what that term means.

Am I an environmentalist because I have taken an interest in Nassau Lake, tried to change our company product line and processes in a more sustainable direction, and make everyday choices to redirect my consumer choices away from fossil fuel-based products? I don't know.

I do know the lake experience has helped me think differently.

Maybe some environmentalists would reject the idea of someone in the plastics industry from considering themselves an environmentalist. Maybe I don't fit the images I had carried for so many years, but I no longer accept those images as the sole representation of the word.

The United Nations called climate change the "biggest challenge of our time." A call to preserve as much as survive. The term should not impede any desire to help.

We all need the Earth.

We all love nature.

We all want to do better.

We are all called to be "wagglers."

We are all environmentalists.

Chapter 16

TIME TO GO

Niagara Falls straddles the United States and Canadian border. Established in 1885, Niagara Falls State Park is the oldest state park in the United States.

Niagara Falls is actually made up of three waterfalls: Horseshoe or Canadian Falls, American Falls, and Bridal Veil Falls. The highest point is at 188 feet and the width of all three combined comes to over 3,000 feet. The Falls are a breathtaking view of nature while simultaneously being a renewable source of energy producing enough electricity to power 3.8 million homes. The park and surrounding area are a bevy of activity and life.

Five miles to the east sits Love Canal. The former Superfund site is surrounded by a chain-link fence that runs the entire perimeter. The seven-city block area is no longer on the federal National Priority Superfund list—nor on anyone's destination list.

The two places are so close but so different.

About 3,160 tons of water flow over the Falls every second.[113]

About 21,000 tons of toxic chemicals were dumped in the open Love Canal trench. If you ever find yourself at Niagara Falls on the perch that provides an overwhelming sense of awe at the sheer amount and power of water falling, stand there and count to seven.

The amount of water that falls in seven seconds is how much toxic waste was dumped into the canal five miles away.

Count 15 seconds more to account for the dumping at the landfill in Nassau.

Keep counting. There are 1,300 sites.

It is time. Time to move. When I started this journey, I thought it was about finding facts and assigning responsibility so we could move forward. I thought I was in a maze trying to find a way out. I now realize we are playing a different game.

A maze seems complex but is simple. You find the path out by looking ahead and retracing your steps when you hit a dead end.

Instead, we are playing a game of Go. With only two pieces—black or white—the game appears simple but is wildly complex. The 2,500-year-old board game forces constant thought on every turn weighing countless potential moves and their results as the game moves along. Strategy, learning, and adapting are constant. The game is not linear.

Complexity can make us feel powerless to make change.

What we must do, therefore, is not try to make the complex simple. Instead, we must work to make the complex understandable. As we understand, we take back control of the power we each have. Understanding is an individual action but can lead to collective movement.

As the sands in the hourglass accumulate, it is time to Go. A universal shock event to force action may come too late or not at all. Time to put your sustainability puzzle together to plug into the larger mosaic. Time to get into your boat and move in a sustainable direction in whatever ways you can.

If we don't, Nassau Lake is giving us a vision of the future.

If we don't work to control waste and climate issues, the issues will control us. If we don't fight for clean water, the people of Nassau Lake know it means water filtration systems, increase risk of poor health, a compromised lake, and a decrease in home values. If we don't fight for clean air, the people of Picher, Oklahoma know it means abandoning their homes and history. If we don't fight for clean land, the people of Love Canal know it means relocating after exposure to buried chemicals beneath their feet.

Clean air, water, and lands are a right we should all enjoy. If they are no longer universally free for all, the fight for survival begins and the spiral of political and social issues turns into a tornado ripping through our society.

A different vision emerges when we fight hard enough and use our efforts to create and build on new ideas that view the environment as a primary stakeholder. Top down or bottom up, tangible or intangible, collective or individual actions, regulatory or voluntary action, all are needed to create the transition we want. This is a new and imperfect journey. We are building bridges to the future as we run across them.

The reward for the right kind of actions and direction is abundance. Abundance of clean air, fresh water, biodiversity, nature's beauty and bounty, and a more equal society. Survival and preservation, then, become one and the same thing. The right kind of action is found in knowing our behaviors influence the environment and in turn affect our communities. We need to have compassion and help those who are forced to choose survival. The right direction is found in awareness, tying action to what each of us likes to do, movement, and signaling. Giving ALMS in our own way to the environment is simultaneously loving our neighbor.

My mind goes back to the image that prompted my journey to find the vision of a better future—I returned to the middle of the lake where I had imagined the scene of the girl skiing and the truck carrying its barrels. This time it was the middle of January and I stood on thick ice and gazed at the shoreline.

WHO ARE WE?

Are we the girl skiing who knows nothing? If sustainability awareness and circular thinking are common knowledge, the chances of not knowing drops significantly.

Are we the truck driver who may have suspected something? If lessons of the past are part of our education system and displayed for all to see, the gap between knowing and acting is reduced. When the gap is reduced, so is the potential damage.

Are we the people who filled the barrels? If products and services are designed with the end in mind, there is no waste. If regulation and reporting are in place to support a "no waste" circular economy rooted in an Environmental, Social, and Governance framework, companies will be less tempted to make absolute growth the sole motivator. If sustainability reporting is standardized and mandatory, consuming products and investing in companies that support sustainability grows.

Are we the lake? Are we people who know the truth, educate with patience, are calm when it is hard to be, and resilient to overcome challenges?

I hope you see your own journey to explore—you are the one in the boat.

The lake knew then. The lake knows now. Now you know.

Our job is to spread sustainability to let it grow. The words and actions may fall on deaf ears, prompt dissenting voices, or be met with blank stares. They may also find thirsty listeners, vocal advocates, or wide-eyed enthusiasts. Our goal must remain to educate, to act, and to especially support those passionate in the younger generation who see the environment they will inherit and advocate for immediate action. We don't need everyone to be a green cow to make change. There are signs to help us along the journey.

The "Re" signs of Reduce, Reuse, Recycle have been up for years. They are now being joined by many more "Re's." Responsibility to the next generation. Request recycled content. Require environmental reporting. Rethink systems. Remember the past. Respond when you know. Recognize opportunities. Recruit others. Recall facts. Regulate impacts on the environment. Relay information to others. Recommit when demoralized. Reconsider common choices. Reverse the trend. Respect the environment. Recover waste. Resolve to help.

There are tradeoffs between the environment and economic and social factors in every decision. What tradeoffs are acceptable reflects one's own world view. My hope is these three become equal participants in the process as we move along.

The road less traveled is the one I have sought to find to help people get into their sustainability boats. Sometimes the road most traveled is the least understood, least analyzed.

As it turns out, the road I have traveled was the same road I've been looking for. The road I have been on 5,000 times that runs parallel to the western side of the lake. It's a simple road but wildly complex. Nassau Lake is a complex problem to solve.

The Loeffel Waste Oil Removal and Service Company operated at the landfill site in the 1950s and 1960s. The company was founded by Richard Loeffel. His son Dewey took over the business and the landfill is identified with his name. Richard passed away years ago. Dewey died a few years back.

When did the company know the waste they were receiving would have catastrophic generational consequences? The complaints over many years were a clear indication something was wrong. The fact that chemicals were found on the Loeffel home residence[114] years later suggests they had an incomplete understanding of what they were transporting—if they knew the dangers of the chemicals why bring them home?[115]

The two primary players in my investigation had passed away, but I realized that they were not who I needed answers from. I wanted to know how to prevent this from happening again, not assign absolute blame as I had grown to believe there was plenty of responsibility to go around—some carried more than others. The companies that contracted the landfill to dispose of their waste; the governmental officials who worked on the landfill case over the many years. The only thing I came to know definitively is that the party who knew but did not act was me. It took me 50 years.

Today, fieldwork, data collection, and sampling continue at the landfill and surrounding area. In the years to come, all the information will be compiled into three Remedial Investigation Reports (RI Reports)—one for the landfill, one for the drainageways (the lake), and one for the primary waterway leading away from the landfill. The EPA site states, "an RI Report is an in-depth and comprehensive document that contains all data collected to define the nature and extent of contamination at a Superfund site." The resulting data collected in each investigation is used to develop different clean-up alternatives to reduce potential exposure risks to humans, animals, and plants.[116]

The lake awaits these reports. Waiting is no stranger to Nassau Lake. But waiting is no friend either. The urgency to find a resolution is hard to overstate for this Superfund site and for the 1,300-plus others. About 22% of Americans live within 3 miles of a Superfund site. These people have been, are, and will continue to be affected forever. Waiting dampens investment. Waiting this long feels more like neglecting and forgetting, funneling toward deep-seated distrust and acrimony.

I no longer think the answer to why the lake has been polluted for 60 years a simple one. I do not think it was rooted in malice. I think that although single actions may seem insignificant, they can still be path-dependent to determine our collective fate. I think the ill-effects of the chemicals are far reaching and extend well beyond the map of the dump site and the lake. I think the lake has lessons to teach if we care to listen. I think part of the environmentalism movement is cleaning up toxic waste sites. I think Nassau Lake is a microcosm of our world today: just substitute PCBs in a dump with carbon in the air. I think the lake is a beautiful place to spend time. I think the people who have lived through this, live with this, lost because of this, and fight for the resolution of a contaminated dump site, clean waterways, and a clean lake will never be recognized or compensated to the extent they should be.

Curiosity above all else has driven this journey. Pure curiosity is judgment-free and I've tried to adhere to the purest form. When curiosity is the driver, judgment is suppressed, and clarity of thought is the benefactor. Curiosity led me to new experiences.

New experiences led to new beliefs. New beliefs led to new feelings, thinking, and actions.

You may not think about chemical or carbon dumping and their effects on the environment and society. It's easy to assume the effects are not real or will not affect you. I recommend you visit a Superfund site. Experience the effects of what did happen there. Once you do, you too may be more inclined to think differently.

Are my feelings today, after an 18-month relationship with the lake, still the same? Will this book weather time? I'd like to think so, but I know other things will invade my thoughts. I don't want my feelings to sink like the rocks I threw in the lake as a boy. Rocks that lie with the chemicals. A part of me lies there too. But I'm no longer afraid of the chemicals—I know now how to think about them.

I now have facts to support how I think about my behaviors. The challenge is how to change individual behaviors on a large scale. It takes time, and along the way people will find themselves pulled by the bandits within distracting them away from nature. This is unavoidable. My goal was clear to me now.

Continuing my own education across environmental, social, and governance issues and relaying that to the best of my ability seems to be the way to keep myself and others in their sustainability boats and keep their inner thieves at bay. Education shortens the time between knowing and action and prompts ongoing understanding.

If I want the eastern pines in my yard to continue to sway, the sanctuary in Rachel Carson National Wildlife Refuge to sing, the mountains of Lake Placid to give a rush of joy to the senses, the John Muir Trail to provide guidance, and the Jordan Pond House to offer spectacular views, we must be wary of and take care of Nassau Lake, Love Canal, and Picher, Oklahoma.

If there is one overriding lesson the lake has taught me it is that of reflection. Seeing yourself as a reflection of nature will engage your movements to act on its behalf. I wanted to move in such a way that the lake knew how I felt.

I still was hesitant to make that final leap. I was on the lake but had never been in it. Was I going to jump in? I knew there were some unseen risks due to the chemicals. I knew swimming was not allowed. I also knew how I felt. Getting into the water became something I just had to do.

I stood knee deep in the water. Swim trunks on, ready to dive. I looked around and saw those rounded hills. What had always appeared as interlocking frowns I now saw as interlocking smiles. My body gets acutely cold and hesitant at the prospect of jumping into water regardless of time, temperature, or place. The hesitancy builds all the way up until some instinct within forces me to re-lease. I know I want to jump but I don't, at least not right away. The uncertainty was amplified as I stood in Nassau Lake. A cold chill came over me on that warm day.

"Stay out of the lake." The mantra repeated over decades sounded quietly in my head. I had accepted it unconditionally, ignorantly.

I would stay out no longer.

I had grown to love the lake. To me it represents a town, a

village, a community, a history. I'm proud to be from Nassau.

When we love, we want to touch, hold, hug.

And so, I jumped.

I hope you do too.

EPILOGUE

I sit on the front porch with my mother. The same front porch she sat on as a girl, the same one I did as a boy. We talk for some time, looking out over the same views as whoever sat here prior had done. Our house and the houses up and down the street were built in the 1700s. Old pictures from the library show they are mostly unchanged today.

We look along Elm Street and watch the people, cars, and trucks go by. I walk out to the sidewalk, look left toward the sole traffic light at the main intersection, look right to the old abandoned building, once the site of a grist mill, sitting at the split in the road—each one leading to opposite sides of the lake. The grist mill used the power from Nassau Lake whose waters flowed behind it. The water still flows today.

As I rock back and forth, I think of the Stockbridge–Munsee native Americans, Jonathan Hoag, Martin Van Buren, the million or more travelers who rode the train line in the early 1900s, and my friends and neighbors. All of us have walked or ridden on these streets. The history of Nassau lives in these streets.

I am the first generation who has never seen the lake as it was in its heyday. Stories of the past carry into the future. My fear is that the present story is one of a lake with no hope of recovery, that Nassau Lake is a premonition.

I do not want the story of the lake to become the story of the planet.

Maybe this book can help tell a new story. A precautionary story of the past to chart an actionable, hopeful story for the future.

I tell my mom about my book. She nods and smiles.

Her memory is not what it once was, but when we talk about certain things, her eyes light up and her brain seems intent on pulling out a memory long buried.

I ask her if she ever water skied on the lake.

She nods, looks up at me, and smiles.

APPENDIX #1

20 STATEMENTS TO CONTEMPLATE TO HELP YOU GET INTO YOUR SUSTAINABILITY BOAT

1. Acting sustainably is a means to love thy neighbor.

2. If you're not buying recycled content, you're not recycling.

3. There are ultimately only three options for materials at the end of life: recycle, compost, or landfill. We want to avoid the landfill.

4. Reduce then Reuse then Recycle. In that order.

5. The climate issue is a social justice issue. The least responsible bear the greatest consequences of climate change.

6. Every choice matters.

7. Buy locally or regionally if possible.

8. If you are waiting for someone else to act, it's probably you we are waiting for.

9. If you are waiting for the perfect path, there isn't one.

10. Inaction has a cost.

11. Pollution is a disease with no cure, it can only be prevented.

12. Closing loops must include all four steps: collection at end of life, sortation, re-marketing, and re-selling.

13. Value what you buy.

14. Awareness is a friend to progress.

15. Communicate to continue the dialogue, to exchange ideas, and to inform, not solely to convince.

16. Appreciating your surroundings is a motivation to act.

17. Knowing what we don't want sometimes leads to a clear path to what we do want.

18. The road most traveled can be the one least understood.

19. Think longer term when possible.

20. Actions influence others in hidden ways.

APPENDIX #2
10 DEFINITIONS TO HELP SUSTAINABILITY THINKING

(in order of appearance)

<u>Path Dependence</u>: The outcome of something is dependent on the path of previous outcomes, rather than simply the current situation.

<u>Circular Economy</u>: A system of no waste. All by-products of one process become feedstock for another product.

<u>Life Cycle Analysis</u>: Attempts to provide an objective, scientific measure to assess the environmental impacts associated with various stages of a product's life cycle: sourcing, manufacturing, distribution, use, and recovery.

<u>Inversion</u>: Figure out what you don't want and avoid it. Avoid stupidity rather than seeking brilliance.

<u>Six Capitals</u>: The value of a company can be defined by the total sum of six capitals: financial, manufactured, intellectual, social,

human, natural. The idea is to grow all capitals together and not substitute one for another.

<u>Environmental, Social, Governance (ESG) Initiatives:</u> A framework to evaluate a business's sustainability and ethical impact.

<u>First-Order Thinking</u>: What appears to be the immediate result of taking an action.

<u>Second- and Third-Order Thinking</u>: The process of anticipating the secondary and tertiary implications of first-order decisions.

<u>First-Order Principles</u>: Foundational elements of understanding. They are the original principles from which other things are deduced.

<u>Precautionary Principle</u>: A broad-thinking approach that is characterized by slowing down, exploring a wide range of alternatives, increasing the number of people in the decision-making process, and gathering more complete information before making decisions.

ACKNOWLEDGMENTS

The idea to write this book came from all those who commented on my first book. I will always be grateful for the readers who have taken an interest in this topic.

I am very thankful to all those who provided information and insights through conversations, stories and interviews. They all combined to provide a level of detail I could never have found in print alone. In particular, Kurt Vincent, Don Strevell Junior, Barbara Reina, Robert Nairn, Linda Krzykowski, Dave Fleming, Kelly Travers Main, Ron and Pat Mocerine, and Dave and Rita Labrum helped shape the story.

Many thanks to the people at the Nassau Free Public Library who provided access to old newspapers, pamphlets, pictures, and books. The staff was overtly friendly on multiple trips and helpful just as they were when I was a visitor as a toddler.

Thanks to Tim Testa and Kelly Ragan who were both instrumental in providing an open ear to my ideas and a guiding hand to make them come alive. Jaqueline Kyle was a big help editing the manuscript. Julie Broad and her entire team were great partners on this journey — respectful of the story yet challenging me to make the book the best version of itself. Thank you.

My faith continues to play a major role in my life. Writing about the Nassau Reformed Church and those people who provided guidance at a young age will always be recognized in how I think and write. The congregation at Saint Henry's parish continues that guidance today. I am thankful for all those who continue to influence my faith and perspective.

The people who live near Superfund sites and the people most affected by environmental related issues face unique challenges that many do not. I am thankful to have gained some understanding of the real and potential hardships. Mostly, I am hopeful that I have been able to articulate the issues well enough for others to become aware to the extent they have more compassion for those who struggle, and they decide to act in a positive direction.

Writing about Nassau allowed me a chance to write about my hometown. I am proud to be from Nassau. My immediate childhood neighbors in Nassau — The Conlees, Cosgroves, Mocerines and Coopers — provided a world of freedom, safety and possibilities growing up. My understanding and practice of a strong community comes from these families and this town. Their collective influence is found on the pages of this book.

A big thanks to my family — Ben, Christian, Jonathan, our dog Bear and my wife Melissa. I did not think I would take a dive to writing a second book. I could not have without an oft times unspoken and unannounced commitment of time and travel. Your collective support helped me, motivated me and grounded me. I will always know what's most important because of you.

To my family who grew up with me at 28 Elm Street — Todd, Tara, grandma, grandpa, mom and dad — only now do I fully recognize the foundation of love and trust I lean on everyday was seeded in that house because of you. Forever grateful.

BIBLIOGRAPHY

BOOKS

Attenborough, David. *A Life on Our Planet*. London: Ebury Publishing, 2020.

Bédat, Maxine. *Unraveled*. New York, NY: Penguin Random House Inc., 2021.

Butler, Octavia E. *Parable of the Sower*. New York, NY: Four Walls Eight Windows, 1983.

Carson, Rachel. *Silent Spring*. Boston, MA: Houghton Mifflin, 1962.

Egan, Timothy. *The Big Burn*. Boston, MA: Mariner Books, 2010.

Foster, Lisa D. *Bag Lady*. Winchester: John Hunt Publishing, 2022.

Gates, Bill. *How to Avoid a Climate Disaster*. London: New York, NY: Alfred A. Knopf, 2021.

Gore, Al. *An Inconvenient Truth*. Emmaus, PA: Rodale Inc, 2006.

Hawken, Paul. *Drawdown* London: Penguin, 2018.

Heacox, Kim. *The Only Kayak*. Essex, CT: Lyons Press, 2020.

Huey, Paul R. and Ralph D. Phillips. *The Early History of Nassau Village 1609 to 1830*. A 42-page book made for Nassau Free Library, 1969.

Jamail, Dahr. *The End of Ice*. New York, NY: The New Press, 2020.

Lewis, Sarah E. *The Change Agents*. Self-published, 2021.

McDonough, William and Michael Braungart. *Cradle to Cradle*. New York, NY: North Point Press, 2002.

McDonough, William and Michael Braungart. *The Upcycle*. New York, NY: Farrar, Straus and Giroux, 2013.

Orlean, Susan. *The Library Book*. New York: Simon & Schuster, 2018.

Orwell, George. *1984* London: Secker & Warburg, 1949.

Perkins Marsh, George. *Man and Nature: or Physical Geography Modified by Human Nature* Seattle, WA: University of Washington Press, 2003.

Rather, Dan. *What Unites Us*. Algonquin Books, 2019.

Raworth, Kate. *Doughnut Economics*. London: Random House, 2017.

Stillman, Scott. *Nature's Silent Message*. Amazon Digital Services LLC, 2020.

Stillman, Scott. *Wilderness*. Wild Soul Press, 2018.

Szaky, Tom. *The Future of Packaging*. Oakland, CA: Berrett-Koehler Publishers, 2019.

Vincent, Kurt. *Nassau (Images of America)*. Charleston, SC:

Arcadia Publishing, 2013.

Zinsser, William. *Writing Places*. New York, NY: Harper Academic, 2010.

PUBLICATIONS

Gardiner, Beth. "The Deadly Cost of Dirty Air." In *National Geographic* 239, 4, (2021): 41–67.

Marris, Emma. "America in a New Light." In *National Geographic* 9, (2022): 36–63.

Kunzig, Robert. "The end of trash?" In *National Geographic* 3 (2020)

Parker, Laura. "We made it, we depend on it, we're drowning in it. Plastic." In *National Geographic* 6, (2018): 40–91. June 2018 edition

https://www.nationalgeographic.co.uk/2018/05/we-made-plastic-we-depend-on-it-now-were-drowning-in-it.

"Climate Reality Leadership Corps Training," The Climate Reality Project, online course, https://www.climaterealityproject.org/training.April 27–30, 2021.

"Corporate Sustainability Management: Risk, Profit, and Purpose." Yale School of Management. https://som.yale.edu/executive-education/for-individuals/leadership/corporate-sustainability-management-risk-profit-and-purpose.

"Circular Economy: An Interdisciplinary Approach," Wageningen University & Research, online course, https://www.edx.org/course/circular-economy-an-interdisciplinary-approach.

The Great Mental Models by fs Farnam Street Vol. 1: General Thinking Concepts, Latticework Publishing 2019 Ottawa ON

Other books written by Trent A Romer

Finding Sustainability

What if the foundation of your family business were threatened by something out of your control? What if the livelihood of 70 employees and their families were at stake, as the license to operate your business became called into question? What if 57 years of family history, grown through generations of hard work and sacrifice, were at risk of being lost? What if the reason were actually one with which you fundamentally agreed?

Journey to 8 states, 3 national parks, and 3 countries to experience the life-changing education and adventures that led Trent Romer to finding sustainability for his plastic bag manufacturing business and himself.

Visit www.trentromer.com for more
information on Trent's work.

ENDNOTES

1 "Meet the Eastern White Pine," New England Forestry Foundation, April 23, 2018, https://newenglandforestry.org/2018/04/23/meet-the-eastern-white-pine.

2 "Winter Tree Identification Part II: Evergreen Trees," New York State Parks, March 3, 2015, https://nystateparks.blog/2015/03/03/winter-tree-identification-part-ii-evergreen-trees/.

3 Richard Grant, "Do Trees Talk to Each Other?" *Smithsonian Magazine*, March 2018, https://smithsonianmag.com/science-nature/the-whispering-trees-180968084/.

4 Suzanne Simard, "How trees talk to each other," TED, July 22, 2016, https://ted.com/talks/suzanne_simard_how_trees_talk_to_each_other/up-next.

5 "Our Common Future," World Commission on Environment and Development, March 20, 1987, http://www.un-documents.net/our-common-future.pdf.

6 Jan Kimpen, "How the COVID crisis could spark positive change in healthcare," World Economic Forum, July 31, 2020, https://www.weforum.org/agenda/2020/07/how-the-covid-crisis-could-spark-positive-change-in-healthcare/.

7 "Case Study: Hayman Fire, Hayman, Colorado," American Planning Association, https://www.planning.org/research/postdisaster/casestudies/haymanfire.htm.

8 Nick Popham, "30 years later: Hurricane Andrew creates universal building code for Florida," Spectrum News, August 24, 2022, https://www.baynews9.com/fl/tampa/news/2022/08/24/30-years-later--hurricane-andrew-creates-universal-building-code-for-florida.

9 Lizette Alvarez and Marc Santora, "After Andrew, Florida Changed Its Approach to Hurricanes," *The New York Times*, September 6, 2017, https://www.nytimes.com/2017/09/06/us/hurricane-andrew-miami.html.

10 Kurt Vincent, "All about Nassau, People, Buildings and Memories: Delson's Economy Store," http://nebula.wsimg.com/5bf3ecfe3152603a70f0789742abfffe?AccessKeyId=3150E8AC5058496F1B24&disposition=0&allowori-

gin=1.

11 Eugenia Angulo, "Muir, Roosevelt and the Camping Trip that Saved Nature in the U.S.," OpenMind, August 23, 2019, https://www.bbvaopenmind.com/en/science/environment/muir-roosevelt-and-the-camping-trip-that-saved-nature-in-the-us/.

12 "Theodore Roosevelt and Conservation," National Park Service, November 16, 2017, https://www.nps.gov/thro/learn/historyculture/theodore-roosevelt-and-conservation.htm.

13 Hannah Featherman, "What are the differences between National Parks and National Forests?" National Forest Foundation, https://nationalforests.org/blog/what-are-the-differences-between-national-parks-and-national-forests.

14 Nicholas Hyer, "The Ways of the Stockbridge-Munsee Native American Tribe," University of Wisconsin, https://www3.uwsp.edu/forestry/StuJournals/Documents/NA/nhyer.pdf.

15 "The Different Views of Land," Smithsonian, https://americanindian.si.edu/nk360/manhattan/different-views-land/different-views-land.cshtml. (De Halve Maen 72, no. 4 (Winter 1999): 75–83, reprinted in Margriet Lacy, ed., A Beautiful and Fruitful Place: Selected Rensselaerswijck Papers, vol. 3 (Albany: New Netherland Institute, 2013): 41–48).

16 Paul R. Huey and Ralph D. Phillips, The Early History of Nassau Village, 1609-1830 (Nassau Free Public Library: 1976), Chapter III.

17 Paul R. Huey and Ralph D. Phillips, The Early History of Nassau Village, 1609-1830 (Nassau Free Public Library: 1976), p.32.

18 "Town of Nassau, New York: Celebrating 200 Years of History and Counting," 2006, https://townnassau.digitaltowpath.org:10091/content/History/Home/:field=documents;/content/Documents/File/400.pdf.

19 Michael Cooney, "Albany & Hudson Electric Railway," Upstate Earth, April 21, 2009, https://upstateearth.blogspot.com/2009/04/albany-hudson-electric-railway.html.

20 "Nassau Lake Park", The Berkshire Evening Eagle, Pittsfield Massachusetts, May 8, 1924, pg. 1.

21 "Albany Boy Saved From Drowning in Nassau Lake," The Times Record, Troy, New York, August 14, 1946, p.3.

22 Kurt Vincent, "All About Nassau, People, Buildings and Memories: Nassau Lake's Taverns, Bars and Joints," http://nebula.wsimg.com/10a4f8b821e9df8926722207662f50ff?AccessKeyId=3150E8AC5058496F1B24&disposition=0&alloworigin=1.

23 "Who Discovered Wind Energy?" Inspire Clean Energy, October 7, 2016, https://www.inspirecleanenergy.com/blog/clean-energy-101/who-discovered-wind-energy.

24 George Duval, "When Were Solar Panels Invented?," Semprius, November 4, 2022, https://www.semprius.com/when-were-solar-panels-invented/.

25 Rebecca Lindsey, "Climate Change: Atmospheric Carbon Dioxide," Climate.gov, June 23, 2022, https://www.climate.gov/news-features/understanding-climate/climate-change-atmospheric-carbon-dioxide.

26 "The Warming Effects of the Industrial Revolution," Climate Policy Watcher, February 13, 2023, https://www.climate-policy-watcher.org/global-temperatures/the-warming-effects-of-the-industrial-revolution.html.

27 "Learn about Polychlorinated Biphenyls (PCBs)," EPA, June 5, 2022,

https://www.epa.gov/pcbs/learn-about-polychlorinated-biphenyls-pcbs#healtheffects.

28 Justin McCarthy, "Gallup Vault: Fear and Anxiety During the 1980s AIDS Crisis," Gallup, June 28, 2019, https://news.gallup.com/vault/259643/gallup-vault-fear-anxiety-during-1980s-aids-crises.aspx.

29 Barbara Reina, "Never Quite Clean," Earth Island Journal, February 5, 2021, https://www.earthisland.org/journal/index.php/articles/entry/never-quite-clean-dewey-loeffel-superfund-site/.

30 "Dewey Loeffel Landfill Nassau, New York: Cleanup Activities," EPA, https://cumulis.epa.gov/supercpad/SiteProfiles/index.cfm?fuseaction=second.Cleanup&id=0201218.

31 "Climate Change History," History.com, August 8, 2022, https://www.history.com/topics/natural-disasters-and-environment/history-of-climate-change.

32 "Global Greenhouse Gas Emissions Data," EPA, February 25, 2022, https://www.epa.gov/ghgemissions/global-greenhouse-gas-emissions-data#Trends.

33 "Climate Change Widespread, Rapid, and Intensifying." IPCC. Intergovernmental Panel on Climate Change, August 21, 2021. https://www.ipcc.ch/2021/08/09/ar6-wg1-20210809-pr/.

34 Morteza Taiebat and Ming Xu, "5 charts show how your household drives up global greenhouse gas emissions," PBS, September 21, 2019, https://www.pbs.org/newshour/science/5-charts-show-how-your-household-drives-up-global-greenhouse-gas-emissions.

35 "National Overview: Facts and Figures on Materials, Wastes and Recycling," EPA, December 3, 2022, https://www.epa.gov/facts-and-figures-about-materials-waste-and-recycling/national-overview-facts-and-figures-materials.

36 Pamela Gill Alabaster, "America Recycles Day," Personal Care Products Council, November 15, 2019, https://www.personalcarecouncil.org/perspectives/america-recycles-day/.

37 Maggie Koerth, "The Era Of Easy Recycling May Be Coming To An End," FiveThirtyEight, January 20, 2019, https://fivethirtyeight.com/features/the-era-of-easy-recycling-may-be-coming-to-an-end/.

38 Darrel Moore, "Most alternatives to plastic packaging 'emit more greenhouse gases', report finds," Circular, July 7, 2020, https://www.circularonline.co.uk/news/most-alternatives-to-plastic-packaging-emit-more-greenhouse-gases-report-finds/.

39 Kirk Johnson, "Throwaway Societies of Yesteryear; Past Decades Were the Golden Ages for Waste, Scientist Says," The New York Times, November 22, 2002, https://www.nytimes.com/2002/11/22/nyregion/throwaway-societies-yesteryear-past-decades-were-golden-ages-for-waste-scientist.html.

40 Deanne Toto, "Global PCR markets continue to be affected by supply deficit," Recycling Today, November 10, 2021, https://www.recyclingtoday.com/article/global-pcr-markets-undersupplied-rising-prices/.

41 "The Nutrition Facts Label: Its History, Purpose and Updates," Food Insight, March 9, 2020, https://foodinsight.org/the-nutrition-facts-label-its-history-purpose-and-updates/.

42 "Naked," Lush, https://www.lushusa.com/stories/article_our-values-naked.html.

43 "Our Mission," Spruce, https://www.wearespruce.co/pages/impact.

44 "Reducing the Impact of Wasted Food by Feeding the Soil and Composting," EPA, November 15, 2022, https://www.epa.gov/sustainable-management-food/reducing-impact-wasted-food-feeding-soil-and-composting.

45 "Promoting Sustainable Lifestyles," UN Environment Programme, https://www.unep.org/regions/north-america/regional-initiatives/promoting-sustainable-lifestyles.

46 Ian Tiseo, "Global per capita generation of municipal solid waste by select country 2018," Statista, February 6, 2023, https://www.statista.com/statistics/689809/per-capital-msw-generation-by-country-worldwide/.

47 "50 States of Recycling," Ball, https://www.ball.com/sustainability/real-circularity/50-states-of-recycling.

48 India Berry, "10 Countries Tackling Plastic Pollution," Sustainability, October 27, 2021, https://sustainabilitymag.com/top10/10-countries-tackling-plastic-pollution.

49 Sharon Guynup, "Rachel Carson's 'Silent Spring' 60 years on: Birds still fading from the skies," Mongabay, May 23, 2022, https://news.mongabay.com/2022/05/rachel-carsons-silent-spring-60-years-on-birds-still-fading-from-the-skies/.

50 "Learn about Polychlorinated Biphenyls (PCBs)," EPA, June 5, 2022, https://www.epa.gov/pcbs/learn-about-polychlorinated-biphenyls-pcbs#healtheffects.

51 "Public Health Statement for PCBs," Agency for Toxic Substances and Disease Registry, August 27, 2014, https://wwwn.cdc.gov/TSP/PHS/PHS.aspx?phsid=139&toxid=26#.

52 Naffisah Othman et al., "A Review of Polychlorinated Biphenyls (PCBs) Pollution in the Air: Where and How Much Are We Exposed to?," *International Journal of Environmental Research and Public Health* 19, (2022): 13923, https://mdpi-res.com/d_attachment/ijerph/ijerph-19-13923/article_deploy/ijerph-19-13923-v2.pdf?version=1666871016.

53 "The Origins of EPA," EPA, June 25, 2022, https://www.epa.gov/history/origins-epa.

54 "ATSDR's Substance Priority List," Agency for Toxic Substances and Disease Registry, November 29, 2022, https://www.atsdr.cdc.gov/spl/index.html.

55 "Population Surrounding 1,857 Superfund Remedial Sites," EPA, September 2020, https://www.epa.gov/sites/production/files/2015-09/documents/web-populationrsuperfundsites9.28.15.pdf.

56 "Superfund sites in the United States," Ballotpedia, https://ballotpedia.org/Superfund_sites_in_the_United_States.

57 "Superfund Site Assessment Process," EPA, March 22, 2022, https://www.epa.gov/superfund/superfund-site-assessment-process.

58 Jessica Morrison, "Polluted sites linger under U.S. cleanup program," Chemical & Engineering News, April 3, 2017, https://cen.acs.org/articles/95/i14/Polluted-sites-linger-under-US-clean-up-program.html.

59 "Love Canal," CHEJ, http://chej.org/about-us/story/love-canal/.

60 "Facts about Benzene," CDC, April 4, 2018, https://emergency.cdc.gov/agent/benzene/basics/facts.asp.

61 Allison Herrera, "Quapaw Tribal Citizens Will Receive Equal Payment In Environmental Damage Settlement," KOSU, September 8, 2021, https://www.kosu.org/local-news/2021-09-08/quapaw-tribal-citizens-will-receive-equal-payment-in-environmental-damage-settlement.

62 Tim Kent, "Quapaw Tribe Remedial Efforts at the Tar Creek Superfund Site," Environmental Justice Forum, June 12–13, 2018, https://www.epa.gov/sites/default/files/2018-06/documents/quapaw_tribe_remedial_efforts_at_the_tar_creek_superfund_site.pdf.

63 "Tar Creek Superfund Site," Oklahoma Environmental Quality, https://www.deq.ok.gov/land-protection-division/cleanup-redevelopment/superfund/tar-creek-superfund-site/.

64 Stephanie Buck, "The Oklahoma town that produced most of WWI's bullets is now a poison graveyard," Timeline, August 9, 2017, https://timeline.com/picher-oklahoma-lead-toxic-186e5595232b.

65 Tim Kent, "Quapaw Tribe Remedial Efforts at the Tar Creek Superfund Site," EPA, June 12, 2018, https://www.epa.gov/sites/default/files/2018-06/documents/quapaw_tribe_remedial_efforts_at_the_tar_creek_superfund_site.pdf.

66 Emily Pickrell, "Contaminated Sites Shorten Life Expectancies, Increasing Need For Superfund Clean-Ups," Forbes, May 20, 2021, https://www.forbes.com/sites/uhenergy/2021/05/20/contaminated-sites-shorten-life-expectancies-increasing-need-for-superfund-clean-ups/.

67 "Superfund 35th Anniversary," EPA, https://19january2017snapshot.epa.gov/superfund/superfund-35th-anniversary_.html; Diana Engeman, "Looking Back as We Move Forward: My 25 Years in the Superfund Program," https://gisarab.com/threads/looking-back-as-we-move-forward-my-25-years-in-the-superfund-program.37617/.

68 "Superfund Site Footprints," Socioeconomic Data and Applications Center, NASA, https://sedac.ciesin.columbia.edu/data/collection/superfund.

69 Mark Garcia, "Space Debris and Human Spacecraft," NASA, May 26, 2021, https://www.nasa.gov/mission_pages/station/news/orbital_debris.html.

70 Cheryl Hogue, "Declining funds slow US hazardous waste cleanup," Chemical & Engineering News, February 20, 2021, https://cen.acs.org/environment/pollution/Declining-funds-slow-US-hazardous/99/web/2021/02. (note: need to create an account to view article)

71 "Superfund Underfunded," Environment America, February 10, 2021, https://environmentamerica.org/resources/superfund-underfunded/.

72 Shabbir Ahmad, "Food waste – The 3rd largest emitter of CO2," Voice of Journalists, April 19, 2017, https://www.voj.news/food-waste-the-3rd-largest-emitter-of-co2/.

73 "Poverty Data: Philippines," Asian Development Bank, https://www.adb.org/countries/philippines/poverty.

74 Kare Lema, "Slave to sachets: How poverty worsens the plastics crisis in the Philippines," Reuters, September 3, 2019, https://www.reuters.com/article/us-asia-waste-philippines/slave-to-sachets-how-poverty-worsens-the-plastics-crisis-in-the-philippines-idUSKCN1VO0G3.

75 "Record of Decision: Dewey Loeffel Inactive Hazardous Waste Disposal Site," New York State Department of Health, January 2002, https://www.dec.ny.gov/data/DecDocs/442006/ROD.HW.442006.2002-01-03.

Dewey_Loeffel_OU3.pdf, p.4.

76 "Air, Stream Pollution Being Probed." *The Times Record*, April 15, 1965.

77 "Nassau Co. Cited in Oil Polluting." *The Record*, May 5, 1966.

78 "Troy Feels 'Pure Water' Whip," *The Troy Record*, September 2, 1965. (newspaper.com: must be a member for access).

79 "Dewey Loeffel Landfill Nassau, New York: Cleanup Activities," EPA, https://cumulis.epa.gov/supercpad/SiteProfiles/index.cfm?fuseaction=second.Cleanup&id=0201218.

80 Rebecca Harrington, "The EPA has only banned these 9 chemicals — out of thousands," Insider, February 10, 2016, https://www.businessinsider.com/epa-only-restricts-9-chemicals-2016-2.

81 "Annual CO2 emissions by world region," Our World in Data, 2022, https://ourworldindata.org/grapher/annual-co-emissions-by-region.

82 Rhonda Triller, "Yale professor discusses 'sustainable finance' at High Peaks Impact Awards," Foothills Business Daily, November 19, 2021, https://foothillsbusinessdaily.com/yale-professor-discusses-sustainable-finance-at-high-impact-/.

83 Kathryn Tso, "How much is a ton of carbon dioxide?" Climate, Massachusetts Institute of Technology, December 2, 2020, https://climate.mit.edu/ask-mit/how-much-ton-carbon-dioxide.

84 "Global Temperature," Global Climate Change, NASA, https://climate.nasa.gov/vital-signs/global-temperature/.

85 Bob Berwyn, "Paying for Extreme Weather: Wildfire, Hurricanes, Floods and Droughts Quadrupled in Cost Since 1980," Inside Climate News, August 25, 2020, https://insideclimatenews.org/news/25082020/extreme-weather-costs-wildfire-climate-change.

86 James Bruggers et al., "Your Trash Is Emitting Methane In The Landfill. Here's Why It Matters For The Climate," NPR, July 13, 2021, https://www.npr.org/2021/07/13/1012218119/epa-struggles-to-track-methane-from-landfills-heres-why-it-matters-for-the-clima.

87 Julia Shapero, "Hundreds of temperature records broken as heat wave scorches the U.S.," Axios, July 25, 2022, https://www.axios.com/2022/07/24/heat-wave-temperature-records.

88 "Population Surrounding 1,857 Superfund Remedial Sites," EPA, September 2020, https://www.epa.gov/sites/production/files/2015-09/documents/web-populationrsuperfundsites9.28.15.pdf.

89 "PCBs a forgotten legacy?" UN Environment Programme, https://www.unep.org/explore-topics/chemicals-waste/what-we-do/persistent-organic-pollutants/pcbs-forgotten-legacy.

90 Kenneth C. Crowe II, "Wells contaminated in Nassau from state Superfund site," Times Union, December 7, 2021, https://www.timesunion.com/news/article/Wells-contaminated-in-Nassau-from-state-Superfund-16680000.php.

91 "Microplastics," National Geographic, https://education.nationalgeographic.org/resource/microplastics.

92 Julien Boucher and Damien Friot, "Primary Microplastics in the Oceans," International Union for Conservation of Nature and Natural Resources, 2017, https://portals.iucn.org/library/sites/library/files/documents/2017-002-En.pdf.

93 Lim, XiaoZhi. "Microplastics Are Everywhere - but Are They Harmful?" Nature News. Nature Publishing Group, May 4, 2021. https://www.nature.com/articles/d41586-021-01143-3.

94 Kimberly Amadeo, "Components of GDP Explained," The Balance, January 18, 2022, https://www.thebalancemoney.com/components-of-gdp-explanation-formula-and-chart-3306015.

95 David Hasemyer and Lise Olsen, "A growing toxic threat — made worse by climate change," NBC, September 24, 2020, www.nbcnews.com/specials/superfund-sites-climate-change.

96 Kiah Collier, "EPA: Hurricane Harvey compromised cap on toxic waste site," The Texas Tribune, September 29, 2017, https://www.texastribune.org/2017/09/29/epa-hurricane-harvey-compromised-caps-toxic-waste-site/.

97 Matthew 22:37-39 KJV.

98 "Circular Economy: An Interdisciplinary Approach," Wageningen University & Research, online course, https://www.edx.org/course/circular-economy-an-interdisciplinary-approach.

99 "Climate Reality Leadership Corps Training," The Climate Reality Project, online course, https://www.climaterealityproject.org/training.

100 Michael Moss, "Nudged to the Produce Aisle by a Look in the Mirror," *The New York Times*, August 27, 2013, https://www.nytimes.com/2013/08/28/dining/wooing-us-down-the-produce-aisle.html.

101 Ghislain Dubois et al., "It starts at home? Climate policies targeting household consumption and behavioral decisions are key to low-carbon futures," *Energy Research & Social Science* 52 (June 2019): 144–158, https://www.sciencedirect.com/science/article/pii/S2214629618310314.

102 John Fialka, "The U.S. Is Ignoring the Climate Benefits of Heat Pumps," Scientific American, December 18, 2019, https://www.scientificamerican.com/article/the-u-s-is-ignoring-the-climate-benefits-of-heat-pumps/.

103 Daisy Dunne, "Interactive: What is the climate impact of eating meat and dairy?," Carbon Brief, September 14, 2020, https://interactive.carbonbrief.org/what-is-the-climate-impact-of-eating-meat-and-dairy/.

104 Ian Sample, "The father of climate change," *The Guardian*, June 30, 2005, https://www.theguardian.com/environment/2005/jun/30/climatechange.climatechangeenvironment2.

105 "Municipal Solid Waste Factsheet," Center for Sustainable Systems, University of Michigan, 2021, https://css.umich.edu/publications/factsheets/material-resources/municipal-solid-waste-factsheet.

106 "Onondaga Lake," Department of Environmental Conservation, https://www.dec.ny.gov/lands/72771.html.

107 "Onondaga Lake Cleanup By the Numbers," Onondaga Lake Cleanup, www.lakecleanup.com/progress-news/metrics/.

108 Glenn Coin, "Onondaga Lake's remarkable transformation: Once a cesspool, now at its cleanest in 100 years," Syracuse.com, December 6, 2022, https://www.syracuse.com/news/2022/12/onondaga-lakes-remarkable-transformation-once-a-cesspool-now-at-its-cleanest-in-100-years.html.

109 "Hudson River PCBs Superfund Site: Frequently Asked Questions," EPA, August 4, 2022, https://www.epa.gov/hudsonriverpcbs/frequently-asked-questions#sectionA.

110 John Cannon, "Protected areas now cover nearly 17% of Earth's surface: U.N.

report," Mongabay, May 20, 2021, https://news.mongabay.com/2021/05/protected-areas-now-cover-nearly-17-of-earths-surface-u-n-report/.

111 Matt Lee-Ashley, "How Much Nature Should America Keep?" Center for American Progress, August 6, 2019, https://www.americanprogress.org/article/much-nature-america-keep/.

112 Jeffrey M. Jones, "Four in 10 Americans Say They Are Environmentalists," Gallup, April 21, 2021, https://news.gallup.com/poll/348227/one-four-americans-say-environmentalists.aspx.

113 "Facts about Niagara Falls," Niagara Falls State Park, https://www.niagarafallsstatepark.com/niagara-falls-state-park/amazing-niagara-facts; "Niagara Falls FAQ: Power Generation," NYFalls, https://nyfalls.com/niagara-falls/faq-4/#much.

114 "Superfund Site Information: Route 203," EPA, https://cumulis.epa.gov/supercpad/CurSites/calinfo.cfm?id=0203244.

115 "Route 203," EPA, https://response.epa.gov/site/site_profile.aspx?site_id=14684.

116 "Dewey Loeffel Landfill Nassau, New York: Cleanup Activities," EPA, https://cumulis.epa.gov/supercpad/SiteProfiles/index.cfm?fuseaction=second.Cleanup&id=0201218.

www.ingramcontent.com/pod-product-compliance
Lightning Source LLC
Chambersburg PA
CBHW020328160726

47992CB00004B/1743